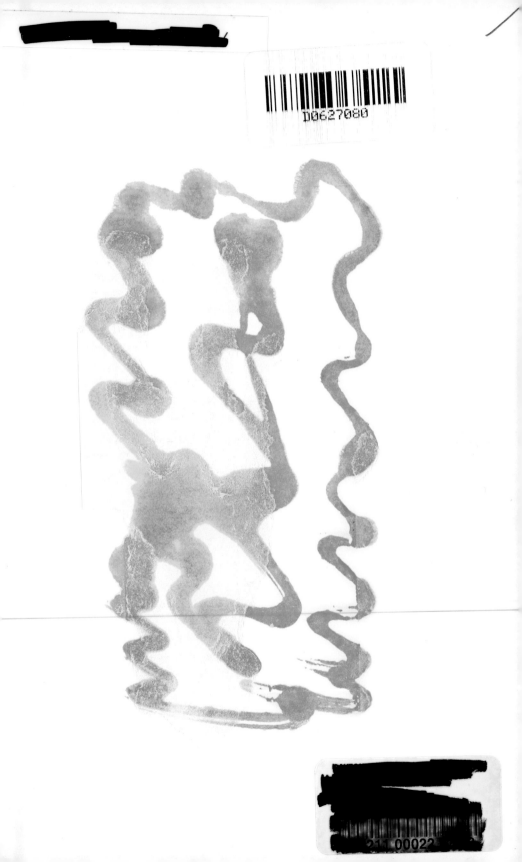

# CENSUS

## 190 YEARS
## OF COUNTING
## AMERICA

*Also by Dan Halacy*

THE COMING AGE OF SOLAR ENERGY
COMPUTERS: *The Machines We Think With*
EARTH, WATER, WIND AND SUN: *The Energy Alternatives*
EARTHQUAKES: *A Natural History*
GENETIC REVOLUTION: *Shaping Life For Tomorrow*
GEOMETRY OF HUNGER
GOVERNMENT BY THE STATES
MAN AND MEMORY: *Breakthrough in the Science of the Human Mind*

# DAN HALACY

# CENSUS

## 190 YEARS OF COUNTING AMERICA

ELSEVIER/NELSON BOOKS
*New York*

Copyright © 1980 by Dan Halacy

All illustrations courtesy of the U.S. Bureau of the Census,
with the exception of:
   p. 41 Library of Congress
   p.92 National Research Council

Library of Congress Cataloguing in Publication Data

Halacy, Daniel Stephen, 1919–
   Census.

   Bibliography: p.
   Includes index.
   1. United States—Census—History.   2. United States.
   Bureau of the Census—History.   I. Title.
HA37.U55H27   1980        353.0081'9        80-10361
ISBN 0-525-66661-3

Published in the United States by Elsevier/Nelson Books,
a division of Elsevier-Dutton Publishing Company, Inc.,
New York. Published simultaneously in Don Mills,
Ontario, by Nelson/Canada.

Printed in the U.S.A. First Edition
10   9   8   7   6   5   4   3   2   1

# CENSUS

## 190 YEARS
## OF COUNTING
## AMERICA

# Contents

# Introduction

If we could first know where we are, and whither we are tending, we could better judge what to do, and how to do it.

*Abraham Lincoln*

CENSUS TAKING is at least 5800 years old. The Babylonians, Egyptians, Chinese, and even the Peruvians beat us to it by many centuries, but America has learned fast. In the last thirty years Bureau of the Census international experts have trained more than 4000 technicians and statisticians from more than ninety nations.

The 1980 census is a "decennial," or ten-year census, the twentieth in an unbroken string of enumerations decreed by the American Constitution itself. Every one of these censuses has been conducted when and as specified, in spite of wars, depressions, and other calamities. The War of 1812 did damage some records, and much of the material from the 1890 census was destroyed in an accidental fire. For 190 years, however, census taking has not only graphed American population on the rise, but has mirrored our change from an agricultural to an industrial economy—and, more recently, to a service-oriented one. It has also reflected our gradual change from a rural nation to one of urban and suburban dwellers.

Ancient census takers used a number of primitive counting

9

methods: pebbles representing fighting men, for example, or grains of corn for citizens. Cowrie shells served as tallies, and so did colored cords. In the biblical censuses, the coins called shekels did double duty in the enumerations Moses ordered; they made up the tithe at the same time they counted the people.

America's early censuses were tallied by clerks with pencils making the time-honored four vertical marks and a slash for the fifth. Census taking sparked a revolution in mechanical counters, and eventually brought on our age of electric and electronic computers. Herman Hollerith, who invented an electromechanical counter for the 1890 census, founded the company we know as IBM.

The census has also been a major factor in the development of statistical sampling techniques, high-speed printing, and such amazing machines as "page turners," microfilm cameras, and FOSDIC, the Film Optical Sensing Device for Input to Computers. FOSDIC machines in 1980 are converting 250 carloads of hand-marked census questionnaires into thousands of reels of computer tape containing billions of pieces of information about America and Americans.

The word census comes from the Roman *censor*, an official responsible for: the registration of citizens, evaluation of property, collection of revenue, the spending of that revenue, and the guarding of public morals.

The U.S. Bureau of the Census does the first task, and something of the second. But it is specifically prohibited from aiding in collecting taxes, and instead of guarding public morals census takers dutifully count households of unmarried couples—with no pointing of fingers.

Those census takers make the fabled couriers of the U.S. Postal Service seem pampered by comparison. They have not only braved a menagerie of animal attacks, but have swum icy rivers and ridden everything from snowmobiles to helicopters and aerial trams to complete their appointed rounds. Some have interviewed nudists, washed diapers, delivered babies, eaten meals with the families they interviewed, and saved lives.

Schoolteachers have traditionally served as census takers. So have housewives, students, and retired men and women. Long ago a Director of the Bureau suggested that letter carriers be made the permanent census enumerators; this has actually come about, but in a way he did not intend. All 1980 questionnaires were delivered to households by mail, and most of them returned in the same way.

America was born of our forefathers' burning desire to be free, to vote for their own leaders, and to follow their own way of life. It is ironic that the census conceived as the means of equitably apportioning Congressional representation now involves more Americans than does any other political process—including voting itself! In all, about 97.5 percent of us have been contacted by the Census Bureau for the 1980 census, about three times as many as will vote.

It is unfortunate, and unfair as well, that the Bureau has been tarred with the same broad brush that blackened the reputation of much of government. Turned off by Watergate, Koreagate, GSA, and other scandals, by rising taxes, and by the prying of many agencies into their private affairs, some Americans complain about answering the questions asked in the census. In actual fact, the Census Bureau has a nearly spotless record of preserving the confidentiality of the information gathered from the people, a record not shared by the Internal Revenue Service, the Social Security Administration, and other agencies.

In all census history, only one employee has ever been found guilty of violating the census law. That was in 1902, when the contents of an industrial report were falsified. A convincing demonstration of Bureau stubbornness in preserving the confidentiality it guarantees was its refusal to give the names and addresses of Japanese-Americans in California to the War Department at the outbreak of World War II. The only complaint in recent times was that of a Washington socialite who felt her confidential phone number had been leaked by a census worker. Careful investigation proved the Bureau blameless. Perhaps more surprising is the other side of the coin. Despite occasional scare campaigns about prying questions on privies, income, mortgages, and so on, in all of census history only two Americans have been fined for failing to answer questions as required by law.

The first American census was taken on the first Monday in August, 1790. Other dates were tried after that, but since 1930 the date has been the first of April. This April Fool's Day date does not reflect a misguided sense of humor in Congress or the Bureau of the Census; it just seems to catch more Americans at home.

When the 1980 census is completed, its initial impact will be on the apportionment of the Congress. This information must be provided to the President by January 1, 1981, so that congressional redistricting can begin. Although Congress created the census, and the Bureau that conducts it, and provides the funds for the task, about the only favored treatment our senators and representatives get is the option of being counted either at their Washington address or in their home states. For those who choose the latter, housing data only is taken for the Washington residence, which is classified as "vacant—usual residence elsewhere."

Population, the first thing to come to our minds at mention of the census, remains the most difficult thing to get an accurate handle on. Time and again experts, including the Bureau of the Census itself, make predictions far off the mark. In 1943, for example, a Bureau publication stated that by 1980, population growth would have stopped altogether at 153 million! Today the Bureau is betting on something closer to 222 million.

In 1790 the first census counted 3,893,635 Americans, including Truelove Sparks, Wanton Bump, and Mercy Pepper. For counting 300 people, a federal marshal or one of his assistants was paid $1. When given the official tally of the 1790 census, President George Washington complained bitterly, because he was sure there were well over 4 million Americans. He was correct, but such "under-enumeration" still seems inevitable today. We have yet to count more than about 97.5 percent, and in 1980 there are in all probability close to 5.5 million "missing Americans."

A miss rate of 2.5 percent is of concern; more critical is the fact that minorities have a much higher rate. Black Americans have suffered most in this regard, and began by being counted as only three-fifths of a man in early censuses. There have been no slaves counted since the 1860 census, but now it is estimated that close to 8 percent of blacks may be missed in the census. Indians, too, are

12

under-counted far more than whites; in early censuses they were not counted at all.

For those who are counted, the census reports much more than mere numbers of people. It sets down where they live and how. It records age and income, sex and employment—or unemployment. Schooling is catalogued too, along with ancestry and the way one gets to work. There were 4 billion facts gathered in 1970; 1980 should turn up many more.

Population and housing are the subjects of the great demographic, or people, censuses. Economic censuses taken in other years cover manufacturing, industry, business, agriculture, construction, and transportation. Ongoing Census Bureau surveys update their information and also cover other areas such as crime.

There are about 12,000 full-time and "permanent part-time" Census Bureau employees. In 1980, however, this force has been swelled by 280,000 "field troops" for the giant task of enumerating about 86 million American households. The first census counted heads for less than a penny each; the 1980 census is costing almost $4 a head.

The two drab Federal buildings in Suitland, Maryland, that house the Bureau of the Census have been unkindly compared with warehouses. There was a time when the census process itself justified a similar appraisal: a huge bin in which to store all the billions of facts turned up by enumerators. But the Bureau, if not its quarters, has for some time had a new image. The Bureau considers itself the largest marketing-research organization in the world. The busiest segment of the field operation is the Data User Services Division, whose chief sees himself as "marketing manager of a plant producing statistics vital to all Americans."

Congress was the first, and for some time, the only, user of census data; today there are tens of thousands of users. Some 39,000 of these are local governments that depend on population and other data for federal revenue sharing. Business, too, depends heavily on information gathered in the census, as is evident by the business representatives who come to the rescue when zealous Administration cost cutters attempt to slash the scope and funding of the census.

13

CENSUS

In 1980 the Census Bureau is publishing more than 2000 reports totaling some 250,000 pages. In addition, more than 2000 reels of computer tape are being packed with far more information than is set down in print, plus nearly 2000 microfilm documents. Altogether, the Bureau publishes enough statistics, tables, charts, graphs, and maps in a single year to fill ten sets of the *Encyclopaedia Britannica.*

Although the Bureau zealously guards the confidentiality of an individual's census records from prying eyes, it makes one important exception. An individual or his legal representative can request from the Personal Census Service Branch proof of birth or other needed information for passports, pensions, job applications, or other reasons. Some 10 million Americans have asked and received such help at minimal cost. There is one other letting down of the confidentiality bars: Census records through the year 1900 are open to the public for the use of researchers, historians, and genealogists. Each census will be opened 72 years later.

Even as they mount the largest census operation in our history, Bureau officials are planning ahead for another major census long urged but only recently authorized. This new challenge is the "quinquennial," or five-year census. "You count pigs every five years. How about equal treatment for humans?" has been the plea for more than a century. The straw that finally broke Congressional resistance was the U.S. Supreme Court decision of 1964, which mandated "one man, one vote." Made law in 1976, the first five-year enumeration will be done in 1985, sandwiched between the other ambitious population and economic censuses the Bureau now regularly conducts, if funds are provided.

A Bureau of the Census staff member recently wrote that "our shadowy existence in a world of passionate anonymity is gone. The press and the public are beating a path to Suitland...." Such popularity is deserved. Both the media and consumers have a stake in the Bureau. Television programming, for example, depends largely on the A.C. Nielsen ratings—which are, in turn, dependent on census data. Not just our TV watching but much of the rest of our life also hinges on census information. If your local government gets any of the $50 billion in revenue up for grabs in 1980, you can thank or blame the census.

The foods you eat, the clothes you wear, and the other goods you buy are all produced and marketed in response to census data of one kind or another. Government unemployment policies, minority programs, parks and other recreation funding, transportation— all depend on the census to some extent.

# 1

# The Census in History

A count of the population and a property evaluation in early Rome.

*Noah Webster*

Man is sometimes described as "the counting animal." The description suggests that other animals do not count, but that is not strictly true. Those who study the habits of birds tell us that some do have the ability to count, and demonstrate it with the way they arrange pebbles and twigs. There is even the remarkable report of one naturalist that certain kinds of birds periodically all fly into the air at once and take a sort of "wing count" to ascertain their population! They then make whatever population adjustments are necessary, either by spreading out, moving closer together, or altering the birth rate. If true, this ornithological census taking is much the same as the kind humans periodically conduct in many countries of the world.

Ancient Babylon seems to have been first to number its people and records discovered in Mesopotamia indicate that primitive head counts began about 3800 B.C. The Babylonian census was taken for purposes of taxation and revenue management; by 2300 B.C. the practice had spread, until each district or region had its own census machinery. Archaeologists have unearthed about

16

30,000 ancient Babylonian census records on clay tablets. The wedge-shaped cuneiform symbols were used to inventory not only households and individuals, but also animals, farm produce, and other goods.

The land of the Pharaohs was probably the next to conduct a census. It is not surprising that Egypt, whose mathematicians and engineers built the great pyramids as early as 2900 B.C., would also feel it necessary to count its people and possessions, and have the ability to do so. The earliest records date from about 2500 B.C. for actual population counts. About three centuries later, detailed maps of the country had been produced using statistics accumulated during census taking. The great Ramses II, who ruled Egypt 1250 years before Christ, refined the administration of his country to the point where geographical and political districts were set up, and accurate, detailed censuses were regularly conducted. These included counts of households and family members as well. In time, the census fell under the control of the Egyptian police department. Then, in the first century B.C., Rome conquered Egypt and took over the census-taking responsibility.

There may have been a Chinese census of sorts as early as 3000 B.C., but only since about 2300 B.C. have there been tax returns and topographical data indicating the existence of formal records. Compounding the research problem is the fact that ancient census takers counted "mouths" instead of heads. The word for mouth is *r'ou,* a word that may also mean just about any kind of person except a baby. The Chinese word for household, *hu,* also means many other things as well. So it is difficult to pinpoint males, females, possessions, or property in ancient Chinese census records.

Although he is not generally remembered as a census taker, Confucius compiled the *Book of Documents* in about 500 B.C. These records included not only population figures but statistics on agriculture, industry, and commerce.

## THE BIBLICAL CENSUSES

The name "wandering Jew" is an accurate description, and not until the Israelites escaped bondage to Egypt did they take an

17

accurate count of themselves. Exodus 30:11–14 describes this first Jewish census:

> And the Lord spake unto Moses, saying,
> When thou takest the sum of the children of Israel after their number, then shall they give every man a ransom for his soul unto the Lord, when thou numberest them; that there be no plague among them, when thou numberest them.
> This they shall give, every one that passeth among them that are numbered, half a shekel after the shekel [about 65 cents] of the sanctuary: an half shekel shall be the offering of the Lord.
> Every one that passeth among them that are numbered, from twenty years old and above, shall give an offering unto the Lord.

The generally given date for this "shekel census" is 1491 B.C. Exodus 38:25–26 tabulates its results:

> And the silver of them that were numbered of the congregation was an hundred talents, and a thousand seven hundred and three-score and fifteen shekels, after the shekel of the sanctuary:
> A bekah [half a shekel] . . . for every one that went to be numbered, from twenty years old and upward, for six hundred and three thousand and five hundred and fifty men.

The first Israelite census is assumed to have been shaped by the Jews' long residence in Egypt, a land well schooled in such enumerations. It is interesting that those enumerated had the responsibility to go and be counted, rather than wait for a census taker to come to them.

The total of the first shekel census came to 603,550. A year later the Lord commanded Moses again (Numbers 1:1–3):

> And the Lord spake unto Moses in the wilderness of Sinai, in the tabernacle of the congregation, on the first day of the second month, in the second year after they were come out of the land of Egypt, saying,
> Take ye the sum of all the congregation of the children of Israel, after their families, by the house of their fathers, with the number of their names, every male by their polls.

From twenty years old and upward, all that are able to go forth to war in Israel: thou and Aaron shall number them by their armies.

Again, the total count came to 603,550.

The third Israelite census was taken in 1452 B.C., on the plains of Moab near Jericho. The count of those over twenty was 601,730, somewhat fewer than 38 years earlier. This decline was probably caused by plagues, fighting, and even fire.

In 1017 B.C., King David carried out another census, this one against the will of the Lord, however. A total of 1,570,000 fighting men was recorded, but 70,000 of them fell because of God's wrath at David. Nevertheless, David did conduct one more census, this one of foreigners in the land. His son, Solomon, conducted a similar one. The drastic results of David's human-inspired census seem to be remembered even in present times. Satan was said to have engineered the fateful Davidian census. As a result, many Christians felt that counting people was sinful, and rebelled against future counts.

## ANCIENT ROME

In the days of Rome's founding, heads were counted; our word *census* comes from the Latin verb *censere*, meaning to estimate. The purpose of the Roman census was to evaluate military strength and provide a basis for taxation, and also to obtain funds for festivals and religious ceremonies, and keep track of newly conquered territories. At one time in Roman history, free Romans, exempted from taxation and military service, were ignored by the censors and not included in censuses.

The Roman census form asked for name and age, class, family position, and personal possessions, including slaves, real estate, and personal property. Foreigners residing in Italy were not enumerated, although their property was. The Roman *censor* was a distinguished official responsible for registering all citizens and evaluating their property. His task did not end there, for he was also charged with collecting taxes and properly spending such revenues. In addition, he was a guardian of public morals. This last duty is reflected in today's meaning of the word "censor."

19

The sixth ruler of Rome, Servius Tullius (578–534 B.C.) is considered to be the founder of the census in that city-state. A simple method of counting men, women, and children was used: each group contributed a different-value coin toward the costs of religious feasts to pagan gods. More money was raised—and more facts were collected—in the requirement of coins in payment at the birth, arrival at manhood, and death of all males. Among the important facts this disclosed was the number of men available for service in the Roman army.

In Tullius' time, the word *lustrum* (for a ceremony of purification or sacrifice) was used for the censuses. About ten censuses were taken between the time of the death of Tullius and the first count taken by the Censorate in 435 B.C., thus a census was taken every decade. The population count in 457 B.C. showed 117,319 Roman citizens. At that time, the Censorate took an action like that just taken by the United States; it ordered a census every five years instead of ten. This will be done in our country commencing in 1985, more than 2400 years after the ancient Roman precedent.

The pressures of expansion, wars, and rebellions were disruptive to Roman record keeping, but in the 232 years from 318 to 86 B.C. censuses were taken on an average of every five and a half years. Registrations of births, of those reaching puberty, and of deaths were required. These data were recorded at temples to the different gods: the goddess Lucina for births, Juventas for puberty, and Libitina for death reports.

As the Roman republic began to fall, so did its census-taking operations. Following a gap of about forty years, Emperor Caesar Augustus revived the census and had three taken during his reign. One was taken in 28 B.C., one shortly before the birth of Christ, and another in A.D. 14. The middle one is of vital importance to the Christian world, of course, because it is recorded in the Bible in the Gospel of St. Luke (2:1–5).

> And it came to pass in those days, that there went out a decree from Caesar Augustus, that all the world should be taxed. (And this taxing was first made when Cyrenius was governor of Syria.)
> And all went to be taxed, everyone into his own city. And Joseph

also went up from Galilee, out of the city of Nazareth, into Judea, unto the city of David, which is called Bethlehem; (because he was of the house and lineage of David:)
To be taxed with Mary his espoused wife, being great with child.

It is interesting to note that Christmas, nearly two thousand years later, is the only day of the year on which the Census Bureau's big electronic computers do not run census data.

## GREECE

Greece's sway in ancient history was short, ending when it was conquered by Rome. Census taking began with the ruler Solon, who lived from 638 to 559 B.C. On taking power in 594, he instituted the census as a means of reforming the tax and landholding laws, probably drawing on ancient Egyptian practices. The only other recorded Greek census came about three centuries later, in 309 B.C., under the reign of Demetrius Phalereus.

## FRANCE

Early censuses in France were the *Polyptiques*, or land-registration documents. One called the *Polyptique de l'Abbé Irmion*, conducted in 806, provided information not only about the land but also about the people living on it. Charlemagne compiled a census termed a *Breviary*, or summary, in 808. Its purpose was to describe the land, people, and property as the *Domesday Book* would do in England 280 years later.

To determine the size of the dowry to be given Queen Jeanne of France upon her marriage to Louis XII, a census was conducted in the fifteenth century in the capital city of Pontoise. French enumerations generally served to guide taxation regulations. By the time of Louis XIV, there were thirty-two provinces in France, each with a "king's man" and his band of assistants, whose tasks included enumerations of population and property so that tax assessments could be made.

The Duke of Saint Simon, in Louis's court, described French

21

censuses as "those impious enumerations which have always out-
raged the Creator and drawn the weight of His hand on those who
have had them made and almost always earned startling punish-
ments." This was a reference to the biblical census of David.

Perhaps because of such divine intervention, and surely because
there were many greedy census takers, the French system broke
down. Records were falsified and in some cases never turned in.
Things were so bad by 1665 that a reform was ordered and thousands of frauds were uncovered and punished. Jean-Baptiste Colbert, the French controller-general, was in charge of the reform.
His intentions were good and he was a capable man, but the system
was so large and so loose that his census was not effective. It is hard
to penetrate the layers of bureaucracy after they become en-
trenched, but Colbert did succeed in instituting accurate statistics
on births, baptisms, and burials, similar to the record-keeping in
England. These have been carried out with only a few lapses until
the present time.

Despite the belief of French cleric François Fenelon that "it is
easy for a king to know the number of his people; he has only to wish
to know," and the boast of French soldier-writer Sébastien de
Vauban that he could accomplish in two days all the enumerations
it might please the King to make of his people, the actual taking of a
census remained a very difficult undertaking.

As late as 1694, a poll tax ran into snags since it was not known
how many people there were in the country. So a formal census
form was drawn up, requiring the census takers to list the number
of towns, villages, hamlets, and parishes in a province, and the
population of each one. In Paris, for example, a lengthy questionnaire also delved into such things as an individual's income and the
taxes he paid. The census takers, however, were not equal to such a
difficult task, and eighty years later Finance Minister Jacques
Necker discovered that there was still little comprehension of
population counts or other needed statistics.

Necker was a brilliant man who pioneered the statistical sampling techniques now so widely used. For example, he first calcula-
ted the number of people in France for each birth that took place.
Then he counted the births for an average year. When the two

numbers were multiplied, Necker announced the official 1781 population for France as 24,802,500. This number was somewhat inaccurate, but Necker had made a big stride in scientific population counting.

## ENGLAND'S DOMESDAY BOOK

The Dark Ages were lit by few statistics from censuses. As Rome and other nations came apart in rebellions and invasions, rulers had more important things to do than count their people. The religious fear of censuses also worked to discourage enumerations. A people who had often counted their numbers in Old Testament times now remembered the fateful "Satanically inspired" census of King David and the plague that ravaged Israel as a result.

Gradually the Dark Ages waned. Some stability was achieved in Europe and in England; trade grew, and there was a need for censuses once more. Ironically, the first of them was inspired by a military conquest. William the Conqueror had need of good statistics on England, so on Christmas Day in A.D. 1085 he set in motion the compiling of records that became known as the Domesday Book.

William's agents canvassed the country, taking information from one man in each hundred—a primitive use of "sampling" techniques. Land descriptions, present and former owners or holders, and the population residing on the land were recorded. Since these sessions were public hearings with the landholders under oath, results were very accurate. The speed of compiling the Domesday census was also remarkable; most of the work was completed in a year. For William the Conqueror that was providential; he died in September of 1087, shortly after seeing the completed Domesday Book.

The Domesday book was a marvelous document, a fitting model for future attempts to count not only goods and lands but people, institutions, and customs, as well as towns and villages. Perhaps its highest tribute lies in the fact that almost three centuries passed before the next English census was ordered. This was done in 1377, by Edward III, and was a rather narrow enumeration that applied only to those paying a poll tax. One reason for ordering the census was the catastrophic effect of the Black Death about midcentury.

Wars and threats of wars for the next several centuries encouraged census taking for keeping track of the number of men of fighting age. Other considerations were kept in mind too, and refinements continued. In 1537, Henry the Eighth ordered the official registration of all deaths, a requirement doubtless brought on by another plague. A few years later the church was ordered to maintain records of baptisms at the local level. However, "morbidity records" were more extensive. By 1600 death rolls were kept in London, and in 1629 women officials counted the dead by sex, estimated their ages and even the causes of death. Such statistics were published weekly as Bills of Mortality. This practice was continued for more than two hundred years.

## THE SCIENCE OF STATISTICS

Government and society had progressed by now to the point where there was not only a need for further sophistication in census techniques but individuals ready to begin this important work. No one nation had a corner on such development, but Italy made an early contribution. In 1515 Niccolo Machiavelli, better known for his classic treatise on power, *The Prince*, wrote a book called *Portraits of France and Germany*. This was a serious analysis of the strength of those countries, including population, the military, commerce, and other resources.

In 1724 England's Thomas Salmon wrote a more comprehensive volume called *The Present State of All Nations*. Twenty-five years later Gottfried Achenwall in Germany wrote similar descriptions of the major nations of Europe. One of Achenwall's claims to fame was first using the word *statistik*, not introduced into English until 1791.

Jean Bodin of France wrote *Six Books on the Commonwealth* in 1576. The last volume included a chapter on the census and listed the following benefits of such a count:

Offers a way of ensuring the defense of the country and of populating the colonies.

Makes clear the legal status of the individual.

Permits knowledge of the people's occupations and social rank.

Affords a means of driving out vagabonds, loafers, ruffians who live in the midst of respectable people.

Provides for the just grievances of the poor against the rich.

Permits levying and collecting equitably the thousands of kinds of imposts.

Enables elimination of extortion by officials.

Puts an end to all rumors, appeasing all complaints, quieting all movements, suppressing all occasion for riot.

John Graunt was born in 1620, the year the *Mayflower* sailed for America. He was a successful London tradesman who became interested in vital statistics, in particular the Bills of Mortality. This information had been compiled for a long time but had merely gathered dust on the shelf. Graunt had an inquisitive mind and soon came across the interesting fact that more boys than girls are born. He worked out the ratio of this difference as 14 to 13.

Graunt found that of 100 people born in a given year, 36 died within 6 years, 24 within 16 years, and so on. With these "vital statistics," Graunt was able to estimate population quite accurately. He also knew why such information was of importance to a nation: Given the population (numbers of male and female, married and single, and soldiers), as well as statistics about cities and business, England could strengthen its trade and government. He reasoned, "If men knew the people they might know the consumption they would make."

Graunt's treatise was titled "Natural and Political Observations . . . made upon the Bills of Mortality." A predictable outcome of his estimate that London's population exceeded that of Paris led to demands in Paris for a more accurate census there.

A colleague of John Graunt was Sir William Petty, a physician who was also a scientist, inventor, musician, Member of Parliament, and Surveyor-General of Ireland. In the last capacity, he published a book called *The Anatomy of Ireland*, which estimated its population for the first time. Petty's book came out in 1672. In 1679 he followed it with *Political Arithmetick*, or "the art of reasoning by figures upon things relating to government." The census was acquiring a scientific following.

One result of the Graunt and Petty work was the follow-up done later by Germany's Johann Peter Sussmilch. Sussmilch participated in the first serious estimate of world population, which for 1800 was set at about one billion.

Sir Edmund Halley is better known for the comet named for him, but in 1693 he published a book with the lengthy and not very exciting title of *An Estimate of the Degree of Mortality of Mankind, drawn from the curious "Tables of the Births and Funerals" at the city of Breslaw, with an Attempt to ascertain the Price of Annuities on Lives.* Translated, this meant that Halley had worked out tables for insurance rates.

In 1753 legislation for a true census was introduced in England's Parliament by Thomas Potter. Not surprisingly, strong voices were raised in opposition to Potter's legislation, for in the minds of some critics, a census would bring on "public misfortune or epidemical distemper" such as the plague that killed the Israelites in David's time. There were other objections as well. Invasion of privacy was feared in those times, too, and the census was branded as "subversive of the last remains of English liberty." Another critic claimed that a census would be a handy catalog of all England's weaknesses for her enemies! Despite the voices raised against it, the census bill passed the House of Commons, but was defeated in the House of Lords.

Despite these setbacks, however, the census was beginning to be appreciated as far more than merely a list of cannon fodder for wars of offense or defense. In 1798, the Reverend Thomas Malthus published his classic *Essay On Population*. This alarming tract stated that though food supplies could only increase by moderate amounts, births could multiply far more rapidly and thus outstrip the land's ability to provide for so many humans.

John Rickan in 1796 had published a paper advocating an accurate census so that businesses and other entities could profit from knowing how many people there were. This paper and Malthus's focused so much attention on population and its importance that in 1800 the Census Act was passed by both Houses and became law. Quite fittingly, John Rickan became first director of the English Census. Also influenced by Malthus's essay, Charles Darwin began work on a theory of evolution stemming from what was popularly called "survival of the fittest."

## TOWARD THE MODERN CENSUS

England conducted its first true census in 1801. Not surprisingly, considering the keen rivalry in the two countries, so did France. Spain, however, had beaten them both with its census in 1798. Norway had taken its first general population count in 1769, although regular census taking did not begin until 1815. Most censuses date from these pioneering efforts. Greece took its first modern census in 1836, Switzerland in 1860, and Italy in 1861.

Russia was a latecomer to accurate census taking, because of the vastness of the land and its long isolation from Europe. The bulk of record-keeping in Russia prior to 1800 was done by police officials, including the secret police. Many people withheld information for fear of being conscripted into the Czarist army, or for other such reasons. In 1802 the Minister of the Interior set up a board to conduct a census of the Russian provinces, but little came of this attempt. In 1810 statistics were placed under the authority of the Ministry of Police, and in 1817 a division was created with that specific responsibility. Still, nothing much happened. Even when the census expert, Belgium's Adolphe Quételet, was hired to set up an organization called the Central Statistical Commission, the Russian government was unsuccessful in carrying it out. Not until 1897 was the first census begun in Russia. Completed in 1905, it showed a population of just under 130 million. A second enumeration was begun in 1913 but the First World War and then the revolution cut such plans short.

It is one thing to count heads and another to consider the act carefully and to write serious papers and books about it. Census organizations, including ours, are fortunate to have a background of several centuries of such thought and publication.

The census is one of man's oldest governmental efforts, and one that has grown in importance with each taking. Although the basics of census taking are not all that different now from what they were in earlier times, the scope and the sophistication of enumerations have changed greatly. No longer are censuses taken principally for the purpose of drafting an army for fighting wars, or for assessing taxes, as was done in the time of Mary and Joseph. And no longer do cowrie shells or four straight lines and a slash serve for counting. Today census taking is a global affair, made accurate by very advanced technologies. This is most appropriate, for the census for its part has aided in the development of those technologies. Far back in history, and as far ahead as we can look into the future, the census is there. For a counting animal, that is only natural.

# 2
# The Census in America

A people who instituted the statistics of their country on the very day when they founded their government, and who regulated by the same instrument the census of inhabitants, their civil and political rights, and the destinies of the nation.

*Moreau de Jonnes*
*French statistician*

The United States was unique in several ways, including the fact that the new nation called for a census almost as a first order of business. We were new and we were small. We were proud of our growth and highly motivated to publish numbers proving it. We had precedent, too, for even before the Constitutional Convention, where our charter was drawn and the census ordered in 1786, a total of 39 censuses had already been taken in America in the 13 colonies.

Ironically, Mother England (which would not conduct a formal census of her own until 1801) was responsible for the American Colonial censuses. The British Board of Trade required population and other information so that it could properly administer the colonies.

The business of counting Americans actually began even before these English censuses in the New World; King Philip II of Spain ordered the first census in North America. This count came in 1577 in Mexico. Philip, as an "absentee landlord," had the census taken for much the same reason the British Board of Trade later ordered the American colonial censuses. Philip's Spanish overlords gave the job to the Indians themselves, and the resulting excellent—and artistic—census can still be seen in the Latin-American Library at the University of Texas at Austin.

South American census taking antedates that in North America. The Spanish Viceroy Don Pedro da la Fasca had censuses taken in Peru in 1548 and 1606. And surviving records of pre-Columbian Peruvian history show that censuses were taken for the Incan Emperor Sinchi Roca. Long before Pizarro conquered Peru, statistics (including a count of 200,000 fighting men) were being collected. These tallies were made not in writing but with *quipus*, braided cords of various colors. The colors represented people, gold and silver, and commodities; knots in the *quipus* accurately counted the numbers involved.

## THE COLONIAL CENSUSES

The first English colony to take a census was Virginia, in 1624. Not until 1698 did the second colonial census take place, however. New York, which included part of what is now Vermont, counted 18,067 citizens. Next came Rhode Island in 1708 with 7,181; Maryland in 1712 with a whopping 46,073; New Jersey in 1726 with 32,442; Connecticut in 1755 with 130,612; Massachusetts in 1764 with 269,711; and New Hampshire in 1767 with 52,700.

Although Indians would not be included in early United States censuses, many Colonial censuses did include the red men whose land this was. For example, Rhode Island's 1730 census counted 985 Indians. Massachusetts also included Indians in its tallies. Negroes, too, were counted by some of the colonies, and in 1712 Maryland reported 8,330 in a total population of 46,073. The census, then, was quite familiar to the founding fathers when it was time to take one for their new nation.

## DESIGNING THE U.S. CENSUS

Debts incurred in the Revolutionary War hastened the ordering of a standard form of census. A census of the colonies had been ordered, but some of them never complied, and the rest did so in different ways. As a result, the payment of state contributions to government dragged on for years. The Articles of Confederation had contained no mention of a census to be taken by the new states, and when the Constitutional Convention met in Philadelphia in 1787, it was obvious that instead of patching up the nearly useless Articles, the delegates faced the job of drafting a new Constitution, with some workable plan for apportioning the legislature. More important even than the levying of charges on individual states to pay for government was the matter of how many representatives each state would get, and on what basis it would get them. One of the first suggestions was that a state's representation be in proportion to its population. Furthermore, five slaves would count as three "free men." (Ironically, Southerners wanted a full count for blacks, since they had the most slaves!)

Patrick Henry wanted voting strength in Congress to be based on the number of *white* inhabitants in each colony. Others wanted the value of property to be considered along with population. Neither of these plans was adopted because of a lack of uniformity in the method of census taking in different colonies. The thirteen original states had each been given one vote for lack of some better way of apportionment. A later suggestion was made that not only population but wealth also be included in determining representation. However, this change was defeated and population was left as the determining factor. And population was to be established by an accurate census, taken in the same manner in each state.

Thus, Article I, Section 2 of the Constitution reads:

> Representatives and direct Taxes shall be apportioned among the several States which may be included within this Union, according to their respective Numbers, which shall be determined by adding to the whole Number of free Persons, including those bound to Service for a Term of Years, and excluding Indians not taxed, three-fifths of all other Persons. The actual enumeration shall be made within three years after the first Meeting of the Congress of the United States, and within every subsequent Term of ten Years, in such Manner as they shall by Law direct. The Number of Representatives shall not exceed one for every thirty Thousand, but each State shall have at Least one Representative; and until such

31

enumeration is made, the State of New Hampshire shall be entitled to choose three, Massachusetts eight, Rhode Island and Providence Plantations one, Connecticut five, New York six, Virginia ten, North Carolina five, South Carolina five, and Georgia three.

These numbers were arrived at only after much argument and horse-trading among the delegates, and some of the more populous states, such as Massachusetts, Pennsylvania, and Virginia, were shortchanged slightly. However, this was a trivial detail that would soon be set right. In the meantime, the *Federalist* papers pointed to the brilliant balance in Article I, Section 2, ensuring an accurate census:

> Were their share of representation alone to be governed by this rule, they would have an interest in exaggerating their inhabitants. Were the rule to decide their share of taxation alone, a contrary temptation would prevail. By extending the rule to both objects, the States will have opposite interests, which will control and balance each other, and produce the requisite impartiality.

Today the situation is quite different, and there *is* a temptation to exaggerate, since this results not only in increased congressional representation but more revenue-sharing money as well!

The Constitution mandated the most bareboned of censuses. It required only a counting of free men, slaves, and those Indians off reservations and paying taxes to the white man's government. "Indians not taxed" were not to be counted either. If this seems a less-than-accurate method, remember that white men were still battling with hostile Indians in some areas; in trying to count heads, enumerators might lose scalps.

James Madison was among the leaders who thought the census should be more definitive; he proposed that one of the questions asked on the census should be "The number of persons employed in the various arts and professions carried on in the United States." Madison pointed out that information beyond mere population would enable Congress to pass more beneficial laws. Madison said that it was necessary to know the description of the several classes into which the community was divided so as to make proper provision for agricultural, commercial, and manufacturing interests. He therefore drafted a census schedule that listed thirty occupations, but critics pointed out that many Americans worked at several different occupations during the year, and that it would be difficult to put everyone into a specific category.

What finally emerged in 1790 from Congress was a census form with only five questions: Free white males 16 years and older, including heads of families; free white males under 16 years; free white females, including heads of families; all other free persons; and slaves.

## COUNTING THE FIRST 4 MILLION AMERICANS

The first census could not rightly even be called a census, for that word was not used in the act providing for it. Furthermore, the Congress in its Second Session had to pass a bill specifying just how the enumeration would be conducted. This legislation became law on March 1, 1790, when President George Washington signed it. Enumeration was to begin on the first Monday in August, 1790, and the counting was to be completed within 9 months, or by May 1, 1791. Two states were given extra time at the outset: Rhode Island, which did not ratify the Constitution until 1790; and Vermont, which did not become a state until after the census had begun. United States marshals were named as official census agents. They were authorized to appoint as many assistants as needed, and assign them to the various enumeration districts. To speed the process, Congress decreed that any person refusing to cooperate with a marshal or an assistant on matters of the census would be fined the sum of $20—a respectable sum in those days.

Thomas Jefferson, Secretary of State under President George Washington, was formally in charge of the census. His role in the actual operation was minimal, but he did instruct the governors of the states as to the Constitutional Article mandating the census, and he also asked the Governor of the Southwest Territory to conduct "as good a census as possible under the circumstances." Since the Northwest Territory was involved in constant Indian battles, Jefferson did not add to its woes with a similar request.

The 1790 census was a bargain—it cost only about $44,000! The

| DISTICTS | Free white Males of 16 years and upwards, including heads of families. | Free white Males under sixteen years. | Free white Females, including heads of families. | All other free persons. | Slaves. | Total. |
|---|---|---|---|---|---|---|
| *Vermont* | 22435 | 22328 | 40505 | 255 | 16 | 85539 |
| *N. Hampſhire* | 36086 | 34851 | 70160 | 630 | 158 | 141885 |
| *Maine* | 24384 | 24748 | 46870 | 538 | NONE | 96540 |
| *Maſſachuſetts* | 95453 | 87289 | 190582 | 5463 | NONE | 378787 |
| *Rhode Iſland* | 16019 | 15799 | 32652 | 3407 | 948 | 68825 |
| *Connecticut* | 60523 | 54403 | 117448 | 2808 | 2764 | 237946 |
| *New York* | 83700 | 78122 | 152320 | 4654 | 21324 | 340120 |
| *New Jerſey* | 45251 | 41416 | 83287 | 2762 | 11423 | 184139 |
| *Pennſylvania* | 110788 | 106948 | 206363 | 6537 | 3737 | 434373 |
| *Delaware* | 11783 | 12143 | 22384 | 3899 | 8887 | 59094 |
| *Maryland* | 55915 | 51339 | 101395 | 8043 | 103036 | 319728 |
| *Virginia* | 110936 | 116135 | 215046 | 12866 | 292627 | 747610 |
| *Kentucky* | 15154 | 17057 | 28922 | 114 | 12430 | 73677 |
| *N. Carolina* | 69988 | 77506 | 140710 | 4975 | 100572 | 393751 |
| *S. Carolina* | 35576 | 37722 | 66880 | 1801 | 107094 | 249073 |
| *Georgia* | 13103 | 14044 | 25739 | 398 | 29264 | 82548 |
| | 807094 | 791850 | 1541263 | 59150 | 694280 | 3893635 |

| Total number of Inhabitants of the United States excluſive of S. Weſtern and N. Territory. | Free white Males of 21 years and upwards. | Free Males under 21 years of age. | Free white Females | All other Perſons. | Slaves. | Total |
|---|---|---|---|---|---|---|
| *S. W. territory* | 6271 | 10277 | 15365 | 361 | 3417 | 35691 |
| *N. Ditto* | — | — | — | — | — | — |

The first census, taken in 1790, listed us in only five categories, and totaled out our population at just under 4 million.

17 marshals were paid from $100 to $500, depending on the size of the state in which they performed their duties. Assistants received $1 for each 300 people counted in cities and towns of more than 5000 people, $1 for each 150 people in county districts, and $1 for each 50 in areas of sparse population. As a result of this penny-pinching pay scale, marshals often had great difficulty in hiring assistants. South Carolina had such a hard time it petitioned not only for an extension in time, but for a raise in pay for assistants. Only the extension was granted.

The marshals and assistants had their hands—and feet—full. Roads ranged from poor to nonexistent, and hostile Indians might be lurking anywhere. Many citizens still recalled the nosy agents of the British Crown, and others quoted the Bible to prove they would be smitten down by the Lord with plague, as in David's time. America was not nearly the size it is today, of course. Nevertheless, there was an enormous amount of land, almost 900,000 square miles of it, stretching from the Atlantic coast to St. Louis and the Southwest and Northwest Territories beyond. There were 600 assistant marshals hired for the first census.

Marshals in all states but Massachusetts had to provide not only their own pens and paper, they also had to make up the forms themselves. Given this initiative, they produced a great variety of reports, from small slips of paper only four inches wide to some that were three feet. The format and bindings of the final reports were also highly individual efforts, from workaday covers of newspaper to one elegantly done up in pink orchid wallpaper.

Boston, with its long experience in census taking, completed its count of 18,038 inhabitants in just 20 days. By the end of the specified nine months, most of the nation's counting had been completed. But South Carolina, Rhode Island, and Vermont had been allowed extensions for various reasons, and not until October 25, 1791, did President Washington report to Congress that the census was complete. On October 27 he sent the results from all the states except South Carolina, which sent in its returns in March, 1792. South Carolina guarded against further delays by sending not one but three copies of the finished product: One by ship to New York, another by ship to Philadelphia, and a third copy by surface mail.

| An Enumeration of the Inhabitants of the town of *Boston*. | | | | |
| Names of Heads of Families. | Free white Males of 16 years old, and upwards. | Free white Males, under 16 years. | Free white Females. | All other free Persons. | Slaves. |
| --- | --- | --- | --- | --- | --- |
| *John Hancock* | 2 | .. | 3 | 4 | . |
| *Samuel Adams* | 1 | 1 | 3 | . | " |
| *James Bowdoin* | 3 | 1 | 5 | 1 | . |

*An early census heads up its list of Boston citizens with three illustrious names: John Hancock, Samuel Adams, and James Bowdoin.*

General Washington had made the informal prediction that the total count would not reach 4 million, and he was correct. He had also said that he knew the tally would be much less than the actual number of Americans, because of a fear by many people of such counting. But at last the census was complete and the following tabulation reported:

| | |
| --- | --- |
| Free white males of 16 years and upwards, including heads of families | 813,365 |
| Free white males under 16 years | 802,127 |
| Free white females, including heads of families | 1,556,628 |
| All other free persons | 59,511 |
| Slaves | 697,697 |

Adding those counted in the Territories, the total number of Americans in 1790 came to 3,929,326. There were inevitable errors, such as the first report of slaves in Vermont as 16 being corrected to 17—when there never had been any slaves in that state! However, Thomas Jefferson, who had guided the census effort, wrote the following letter to a friend:

> I enclose you also a copy of our census, written in black ink so far as we have actual returns, and supplied by conjecture in red ink, where we have no returns; but the conjectures are known to be very near the truth. Making very small allowance for omissions, which we know to have been very great, we are certainly above four millions, probably about four millions one hundred thousand.

## WHAT'S IN A NAME?

If the names taken in the 1980 census were posted in a public place, that act would be in violation of Federal law and liable to a fine or imprisonment, or both. In 1790, names of household heads were posted for all to see and correct (Thomas Jefferson took this opportunity to add his name in Philadelphia). And such names as were taken! Boston Frog was counted, and so were Booze Still and Over Jordan. Joseph Scolds was, too, along with Thomas Simmers, Truelove Sparks, Sermon Coffin, Sarah Simpers, Wanton Bump, Mercy Pepper, and Hannah Cheese.

Last names included Cusser, Dunce, Madsavage, Rascal, Soup, Tripe, Vinegar, Pockerpine, Drip, Fryover, Hungerpealer, and Slappy. Where they had come by such interesting names is a mystery; perhaps they were a result of the adventurous, reckless spirit of the times. Other names were Fish, Trout, Kidney, Ham, Lamb, Melon, Feather, Lace, and Bonnet. Also Hash, Grapewine, Redsleeves, and Bodkin, plus Pilgrims, Goodfellows, Swindles, Barefoot, Witty, Pettyfool, Booby, Devotion, Flurry, Miserly, Underhand, Gripe, and Howls! There were Preachers and Rectors, but also Sinners and Parodys as well, along with Treason, Hearse, Tombs, Moregraves, Murder, and Demon. Mr. House was counted, and so was Mr. Lot. And Barns, Stable, Buttery, Ten-penny, and Thickpenny. Most of these strange names have not held up well, and are seldom seen in today's censuses.

In all, there were 27,337 different family names listed by the census takers in those states whose records still exist. Of these, 11,934 were one of a kind. At the other extreme were old reliable names like Smith, with 5,932 families reported, followed by Brown with 3,358. Johnson was third with 2,646. Today Smith is still the most popular name, but Brown has lost out to Johnson.

Nearly half the total different names were recorded in Pennsylvania; the result of that state's being the original Colonial melting pot, with a very large German population and many other nationalities as well. Massachusetts, with a population almost as large, reported only 4,452 names, compared with Pennsylvania's 13,883. This was because most of those who settled in Massachusetts came from the British Isles.

Most Americans live in cities in 1980, but in 1790 only a tiny fraction were city-dwellers. Cities were not yet popular places to live. New York, as today, was the largest of American cities, with a population of 33,131. Philadelphia was next with 28,522. Third place went to Boston with 16,038. Charleston, South Carolina, at 16,359 was fourth, and Baltimore fifth with 13,503 inhabitants. Only 3.3 percent of Americans lived in "urban areas"—cities with 8,000 or more population.

We tend to look back at the 1790 census as a quaint undertaking of limited use. But in its time that pioneer task of counting Americans was hailed as a success beyond the hopes of most of its planners. Perhaps the greatest tribute of all came from England, where, in 1793, a Lombard Street printer named J. Phillips published the American census in its entirety.

## THE FIRST SEVENTY YEARS

For the 1800 census, the American Philosophical Society, through its president Thomas Jefferson, asked Congress to include questions on occupation, marital status, and country of birth. Not yet ready for such a drastic change, the legislators nevertheless bravely requested the ages of females counted in the census, a question that must have met with some resistance. Population had increased about a third to 5.3 million, and the number of enumerators employed in counting the census likewise climbed to 900 from the 650 of a decade earlier. The cost per head counted jumped only about a tenth of a cent, however.

Trouble with England triggered the first "Census of Manufactures" in 1810, as Americans began to appreciate the importance of the information Madison had suggested. When the trouble led to war, the fighting resulted in destruction of some earlier census records. The population had climbed to 7.2 million, and 210 more enumerators were needed. The cost of the census was more than double that of 1790, but for that extra money, census personnel produced a total of 469 pages of reports, up from only 74 in 1800.

The Census of Manufactures had not been responded to well in 1810. Neither was it in 1820, since businessmen feared the loss of trade secrets and other proprietary information, and in 1830 that census was dropped because of such opposition to it. But questions about deaf-mutes and the blind were added. The population was now almost 13 million, about triple that of the first census. A welcome innovation was the introduction of printed schedules of uniform size.

By 1840 there was enough pioneering spirit in Congress to increase considerably the amount of information sought for the census, and the questions were again greatly expanded. Census takers asked about insane and idiotic persons, about occupations, literacy, and military pensioners. Not only was the population census expanded in scope, but censuses of agriculture, mineral industries, and fisheries were also conducted. Unfortunately, the world was not yet ready for such an ambitious census.

The 1840 effort was flawed with errors stemming from antiquated methods, and both individuals and businesses offered strong resistance to questions they thought prying. One newspaper in the South thought so poorly of the idea of soliciting information on industry and commerce that it questioned the "dignity and high functions of the Federal Government" for pursuing such petty investigations! The population had climbed to 17.1 million, and it took 2167 enumerators to count them (at 4.8 cents a head). There was an office force of 28 in Washington, and 1465 pages of reports were published.

For the 1850 census, an embarrassed Congress made some improvements. One was legislation ensuring future censuses even if no new law was passed every ten years and censuses of 1850, 1860, and 1870 were all taken under this law. There were other changes as well. The Secretary of the Interior, rather than the Secretary of State, appointed an official later called the Superintendent of the Census. This Superintendent supervised the United States marshals, who still organized the actual enumeration.

Other innovations included the sending of questionnaires to Washington, D.C., for tabulation. The questions asked were more numerous too. They included "social questions" about taxes, public debt, education, the handicapped, real-estate values, crime, libraries, newspapers, and even religion.

The Mexican War had recently ended; America was still growing rapidly. Sixty years after the first census the population had grown to a whopping 23.2 million; our nation was no longer small. The army of census takers totaled 3,231, and there were 160 people working in the central office; costs had gone to a bit over 6 cents a head.

*In 1850, an enumerator at Marshfield, Massachussetts, noted that Senator Daniel Webster was sixty-eight years old.*

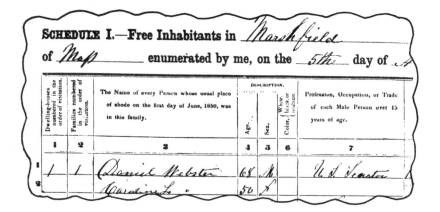

**THE GREAT TRIBULATION.**

Census Marshal.—"I jist want to know how many of yez is deaf, dumb, blind, insane and idiotic—likewise how many convicts there is in the family—what all your ages are, especially the old woman and the young ladies—and how many dollars the old gentleman is worth!"

[Tremendous sensation all round the table.]

*As early as 1860, the census appeared to many people as nosey; here a cartoon from* The Saturday Evening Post *makes fun of its "impertinent" questions.*

In 1860 the population was 31.4 million, with 4,417 enumerators counting them. Instead of six questions, there were six separate census questionnaires in 1860, with a total of 142 items, which included not only population but health, mortality, pauperism, literacy, income, occupation, agriculture, business, banking, insurance, transportation, libraries, newspapers, crime, and religion.

There was an innovation in the 1860 census with regard to its printing. Where earlier censuses had all been printed by private contractors, that of 1860 was done in the newly established Government Printing Office.

The 1860 enumeration was hailed by government as the greatest yet conducted by any nation, and surely there was a wealth of information in it. But it was still too ambitious for the tabulation methods available. Again the census was filled with errors, and it was so slow to process that the 1870 census had been taken before all of the 1860 statistics were published! A Census Bureau historian later wrote that only the population (31.4 million) was an accurate assessment of the state of the nation in 1860!

## THE UNITED STATES ON THE EVE OF WAR

Joseph C. G. Kennedy, Superintendent of the 1860 census, filed an excellent report of that undertaking, at one point describing the decade's progress as follows:

The figures which we have given make it appear that during the decade from 1850 to 1860 our population, in the aggregate, has increased more than thirty-five per cent. More than fifty millions of acres of land were brought into cultivation. The productions of agriculture multiplied in ratio greater than the population. The products of manufacture increased nine hundred millions of dollars, or at the rate of eighty-six per cent. The banking capital ran up from $227,469,074 in 1850, to $421,880,095 in 1860, while the circulating currency was augmented $52,089,560. The amount of insurances increased about $311,000,000. More than 22,000 miles of railroad were completed, and the capital involved increased from $296,640,148 in 1850, to $1,151,560,829 in 1860; while to indicate on the map of our country the lines of telegraph would be to represent the web of the spider over its entire surface. Our internal and foreign trade kept pace with our advance in production and increase of capital. Education, free to a great extent, has been made more accessible, and crime has rather diminished. We experienced no effects of wide-spread pestilence, and our country seemed the chosen abode of prosperity and peace. . . .

Kennedy also included a long section on slavery and the race question, from which the following is excerpted:

There are now in the United States about 4,000,000 slaves. They have advanced to that vast number from about 700,000 in 1790. . . .

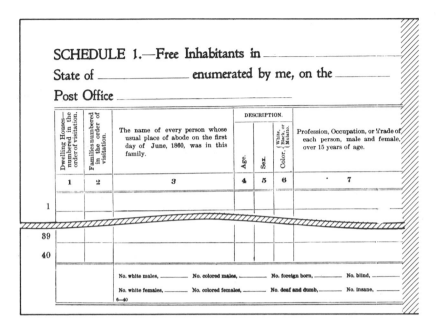

SCHEDULE 1.—Free Inhabitants in _____

State of _____ enumerated by me, on the _____

Post Office _____

| Dwelling Houses—numbered in the order of visitation. | Families numbered in the order of visitation. | The name of every person whose usual place of abode on the first day of June, 1860, was in this family. | DESCRIPTION. | | | Profession, Occupation, or Trade of each person, male and female, over 15 years of age. |
| | | | Age. | Sex. | White, Black, or Mulatto. Color. | |
| 1 | 2 | 3 | 4 | 5 | 6 | 7 |
| 1 | | | | | | |
| 39 | | | | | | |
| 40 | | | | | | |

No. white males, _____ No. colored males, _____ No. foreign born, _____ No. blind, _____

No. white females, _____ No. colored females, _____ No. deaf and dumb, _____ No. insane, _____

6—40

*By 1860, the census had begun to collect information that went beyond the mere number of qualified voters.*

Shortly there would be a war between those prosperous states which would put an end to slavery.

From 1790 to 1860 eight censuses had been taken in the United States, and census taking grew as the land and the people did. In 1860 there was more than 3½ times as much land to cover; the population had increased even more than that. Fewer than 4 million inhabitants had been counted in 1790; the 1860 census showed more than 31 million in a nation less than a century old. And the thirteen original states had grown to thirty-four when Kansas was admitted to the United States in 1861.

Census statisticians were amazed at the regularity of population growth with each decade. The average increase was a bit more than one third—34.6 percent, to be exact—and never had this varied more than 2 percent! So regular was the population growth that a prediction made in 1815 for each census through 1860 proved almost exact. The Civil War, however, drastically curtailed population growth in the United States. Superintendent Kennedy's fore-

*Lawyer Abraham Lincoln, his wife, sons, and female servant appeared modestly in this 1860 enumeration.*

*Less easy to recognize in this same census, thirteen-year-old Tom Edison is listed as "Alvah ... Newsboy."*

cast for 1900 was 25 million too high. Even President Abraham Lincoln fell into the trap: he predicted a population of 215 million for 1925, a total we did not reach until fifty years after that date.

The Civil War had another impact on population and the census. By the time of the War, slaves had disappeared in the North, and even in the South the number had dwindled. In the 1790 census, one family in six had held slaves, with an average number of seven. By 1860, only one family in ten held slaves, although the number of slaves had increased to an average of 10 for each slave-holding family. From 1870 on, there were no slaves listed in the census, and a black would never again count for only three fifths of a person. Another statistic derived from the censuses was that only in the decade from 1800 to 1810 did blacks increase in population more rapidly than whites. In that year, the black increase was 37.5 percent, compared to an increase of 36.1 percent for whites.

The census had originally been mandated for apportioning the House of Representatives. In 1790, each of the 105 representatives in Washington spoke for 33,000 people. In 1860, House membership had more than doubled to 241, but by then a congressman had more than 127,000 constituents.

*Census takers once carried badges like those of U.S. marshals.*

## CENSUS TAKING THROUGH 1890

Census takers counted 38.6 million Americans in 1870, and for the first time in history, Indians were counted among them. The 1870 census was also the *last* that was carried out by United States marshals; the next census was conducted by specialized professionals. Congress had created a Census Office within the Department of the Interior, and an official called the Superintendent of the Census. However, both the Census Office and its Superintendent remained *temporary* creations, legislated to be dissolved as soon as the results of the census were published.

We have noted that as the 1870 census got under way, overworked counters and analyzers were still trying to sort out the data from the 1860 effort. It was perhaps this logjam of work that prevented an 1875 census, demanded by many as a fitting centennial celebration. However, the 1880 census was worthy, at least in quantity, of our nation's first hundred years. A major result of the

*A hard-working enumerator notes down the increase in this family's population in the last ten years—a drawing from* Harper's Weekly, *November 19, 1870.*

*Instructions to the census takers who were counting members of various Indian tribes in 1880.*

information collected (in more than 13,000 categories!) was to convince the Congress and high government officials that some better system was needed if the census was to accomplish its mission. The new Census Office hardly got off to a good start either. The pay was abominable—as low as 10 cents for each 100 people counted, and Congress was slow in appropriating even enough to cover this pittance. By 1881 the money ran out, and the tabulating of the census had to be done by hundreds of volunteers.

To be fair, there were some good things about the 1880 census. Three Massachusetts women had petitioned for the right to serve as census takers, and their request was granted. Of the total of 31,382 counters hired, 200 were women. There were almost 1,500 workers in the office staff, and more than 21,000 pages of reports were produced. At a cost of nearly $6 million, the census counted a total population of 50.2 million, with Spanish-Americans counted sepa-

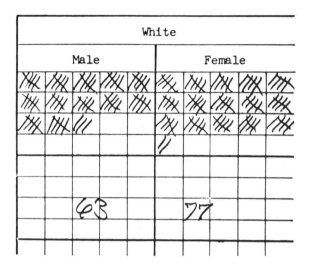

| White | | | | | | | | | |
|---|---|---|---|---|---|---|---|---|---|
| Male | | | | | Female | | | | |
| 63 | | | | | 77 | | | | |

*An early tally sheet.*

rately for the first time. Among the mass of facts and figures reported was the United States fish catch for 1880, a total of 1.7 billion pounds (in 1970 it was 4.9 billion pounds).

The population had outrun old counting methods; the demand for more information from each individual made it obvious that tallying by hand just could not keep up. Inventors came to the rescue, and Herman Hollerith's electric tabulating machinery was first used in the 1890 census. Hollerith, who graduated from Columbia University at the age of 19, went to work for the Census Bureau as the 1880 census was being laboriously counted. So slow was the manual system of tallying (four vertical strokes and a diagonal to indicate a group of five) that the 1880 census was not completed before the 1890 effort was due. Hollerith put his brain to work on the problem at the suggestion of Dr. John Billings, an army doctor who had worked on the statistics of mortality. In 1889, Hollerith entered his electromechanical machine in a census test at St. Louis and won the competition; his equipment was selected for the 1890 census. It was estimated that the new system saved two years' time.

Few people today have ever heard of Herman Hollerith, but almost everyone has heard of the company he founded. Its name is now IBM, and in large part it owes its beginning to the Bureau of the Census.

In spite of the tremendous help from electromechanical counting, the cost of the 1890 census jumped nearly $6 million over 1880, to a total of $11.5 million. The number of enumerators rose to almost 47,000, and the office force more than doubled. However, the information yielded was the most voluminous yet: a total of 26,408 pages of reports. The cost of the census was still only 18 cents per capita, a tremendous bargain for the information produced.

The interest of government in many more areas than merely numbers of people was evident in the questions asked each respondent: address, ability to speak English, diseases, whether he was a renter or an owner, and mortgage information. These social questions gave information on education, health, and residence, and were of value to those attempting to plan for the future.

The 1890 census counted 63 million Americans, and as a result of the census the membership of the House of Representatives grew to 357 and continued to reflect more Congressmen where there were more people. This, of course, was the first responsibility of the census as called for in the Constitution.

## INTO THE TWENTIETH CENTURY

The twelfth decennial census recorded America's entry into the twentieth century. There were 13 million more people to count, but the Hollerith counters (already improved) handled the job well. There were 6,000 more census takers than in 1890, but instead of doubling, as it had historically, the cost of the census increased only a few hundred thousand dollars over 1890. And the cost per head actually *dropped* about 3 cents, the first time a reduction had ever taken place. Even in 1910 the cost was less per capita than it had been in 1890.

National income was more that $19 billion in 1900, and the House of Representatives had grown to 391. Among other statistics was the fact that automobile sales in the nation totaled 4,100 (in 1970 they would be 6,546,800). A darker discovery was the fact that 230 homicides were committed in 1900, a number that would skyrocket to 16,848 by 1970. Statistics presented this way are far less meaningful than when we look at situations closer to home. For example, let's consider Midtown, U.S.A., in 1900. This hypothetical town with a population of 330,435 citizens experienced only one killing in that year. In 1970, when Midtown had grown to 882,609, or less than threefold, there were sixty-five murders!

The most significant census event following the turn of the century was the creation at last of a permanent Bureau of the Census within the Department of Commerce and Labor. This came about in 1902. Although problems remained, the stage was set for an ongoing census-taking organization rather than a spur-of-the-moment effort that would as quickly be disbanded.

However, in 1910, with more than 92 million Americans, the Bureau strained to keep up, even with the new electromechanical counters. In an attempt to improve the situation, a "mail-in"census form was initiated. It was a noble attempt, but Americans were not yet ready for such a streamlined approach. A housewife in Chicago, weary of persistent cold weather and nagging colds, looked at the printed form and thought to herself, "Why should I waste my time answering all these nosy questions?" and dropped the offending paper into the wastebasket. So did a fireman in Tampa, Florida, and a storekeeper in San Diego, California. So did most of the American public. Census questionnaires were still chores, and with no census takers to prod them, people just couldn't be bothered. Returns were so poor that the idea was abandoned for several decades.

*The machine enters the field of census taking—a tabulator helps a clerk total the reports of enumerators.*

On the brighter side, census workers were chosen by qualifying examination for the first time. And the Census Bureau must have been doing *something* right, for state-conducted censuses began to wane in 1914. By 1960 Massachusetts and Kansas would be the last holdouts.

We are a nation proud of milestones, and 1920 was truly a milestone year. The end of World War I was a reason for great rejoicing. So was the fact that the population of the United States had at last—or perhaps so soon—topped 100 million. In fact, there were 106 million Americans counted in the census. More than 87,000 of those people had served as enumerators, and there was an office force of 6,300 in the Bureau of the Census. The cost per head for the census was almost 24 cents, and the total number of pages in the reports published had climbed back up to 14,550, still considerably lower than the 26,408 in 1890.

## THE GREAT DEPRESSION

By 1930, as America sank into the Great Depression, its population reached 123.2 million, an increase of 17 million in a decade, the largest yet recorded. Perhaps because of hard times, census takers grew by only a few hundred, however, as did the office force. In 1929 Congress had passed most of Title 13, United States Code, setting standards which prevail in the Census Bureau today. Confidentiality was further strengthened. And a court decision in 1930 established aid to the individual as the only reason for releasing information about him or her. For example, a state agency could not get into someone's census records in an attempt to remove him from the welfare rolls, but that person himself could request and get copies of census documents that established his citizenship, age, or other needed information.

In 1935 there was a strong plea for a population census every five years rather than ten. The proponents argued that pigs and chickens were counted every five years but not people, because of the Census of Agriculture in 1935. It was indeed true that we knew more about pigs than people. But America was still forty years from changing that.

51

*The 1940 census is proclaimed by President Franklin D. Roosevelt with the words "The prompt, complete, and accurate answering of all official inquiries . . . should be regarded as one of the requirements of good citizenship."*

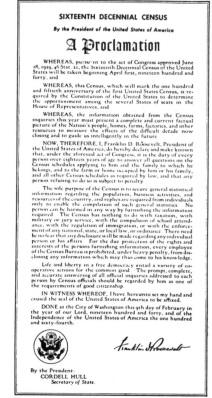

In 1940 there were 132.2 million Americans counted in the census; an increase only about half that of the preceding decade because of the effects on family life of the Depression during the 1930's. Census takers had grown to more than 123,000, however, almost one for each thousand of total population, and the census was now costing more that $67 million, just over 50 cents a head.

Controversy also touched the census. For years Americans had objected to having to tell where they went to church. They had won that battle against the invasion of their privacy, but now they were being asked a question that some thought was even more prying: "Where do you go to the bathroom?" Government planners were interested in knowing how many old-fashioned privies were still in use in America, and so the question was put on the census questionnaire.

Regardless of plumbing facilities, about 82 percent of the population had radios, and most heard Senator Charles Tobey of Vermont urge them to boycott the census form that asked such "snooping" questions. Few people refused to answer, however, and much was learned about America's life-style 150 years after our nation's birth. Average wages were $595 that year, ranging from a low of $218 in Mississippi to a high of $1,170 in Washington, D.C. There were 4,474,000 government employees, more than the nation's population in 1790!

One innovation of the 1940 census was the "sampling" technique. Bright young Bureau statisticians demonstrated that by asking a small percentage of the population certain questions, valid answers could be gained for the whole nation. Of great importance, too, was the beginning of a tremendous amount of work the Bureau of the Census would do for the war effort in compiling information on the labor pool, materials, industries, and so on. Rosie the Riveter's job, and where she worked, depended in part on needs spelled out by the Census studies. So did the cutting of timber and

*A punch card from the 1940 census, describing the age, education, house ownership, race, economic status, and other facts about a South Bend, Indiana, housewife.*

the sawing of lumber for building war plants and Army camps. People and raw materials and facilities were needed to make steel and build Liberty ships. The Bureau of the Census helped put all these things together and to keep track of how the war effort was going.

During the Depression years, unemployment statistics had been collected by WPA workers and published as the Monthly Report on the Labor Force. In 1942, the responsibility for continuing this work was given to the Census Bureau, and in 1947 the name of the report was changed to the Current Population Survey.

## 150 YEARS OF CENSUS TAKING

To commemorate 150 years of census taking, in the midst of World War II, the Bureau of the Census published a booklet titled *Uncle Sam: How He Grew*. Today it is quaint and interesting to read. Included were a number of interesting facts turned up by the census takers:

California and Florida alone had enough orange trees to equal one per United States family in 1940. Nationally, there was one milk cow per person. Longevity statistics showed that only one person in a hundred lived to be a hundred—not counting the 155 legally executed that year. Heart disease killed one person in four.

Among the odd occupations listed by enumerators were: fish-worm rancher, whistle tester, ham sniffer, and egg breaker. Mississippi was 49.5 percent black. Over $1 billion literally went up in smoke that year curling from the ends of 180 billion cigarettes (not yet marked harmful by the Surgeon General) and 7,900,000 cigars. And the beer consumed in America annually would make a river 20 feet deep and 100 yards wide, extending from Bridgeport, Connnecticut to Washington, D.C.!

Under the alarming heading "Growth Will Stop," the editors of *Uncle Sam: How He Grew* made a remarkable prediction:

The Nation's most rapid population growth, proportionately, was 36.4 percent between 1800 and 1810. This rate of increase remained fairly constant until 1860–70. In 1880 it began a steady decline . . . . Authorities estimate that by about 1980 our population growth will have stopped altogether, at a peak of around 153 million.

The Census Bureau writers goofed as badly as Superintendent Kennedy had done in the midst of another war, only in the opposite direction. The United States sailed by the predicted limit of 153 million souls in just 11 years! Such a blunder is funny now, but at the time it was no joke to those who accepted the population projection as accurate. A case in point was the decision of Montgomery Ward to cut back on expansion in view of an expected population leveling-off. Sears, on the other hand, did not believe the projections and continued its growth to reap a much greater profit when population continued to climb.

At midcentury, America's population stood at 151.3 million. The 142,962 enumerators who counted them were paid on a daily basis rather than so much per head, but the Bureau was still approaching the crisis of too much data with methods too slow to handle it properly. A revolution in information handling was needed, and it was about to occur.

## COMPUTER REVOLUTION

In 1950, International Business Machine Corporation (IBM), the company that young Herman Hollerith had founded sixty years earlier, produced its Series 101 electromechanical "sorter-counter." But the computer was also being born. Pioneered as an aid to the war effort in the 1940's, the first computers were monstrosities, but they worked much faster than other calculating machines. Very quickly, electronic tubes and then transistor devices replaced the large electromechanical switches, and by 1951 the first UNIVAC computer had been delivered to the Bureau of the Census. It was used twenty-four hours a day in tabulating returns.

The Bureau developed high-speed printers and equipment for converting punched cards to magnetic tape, and the UNIVAC I was used on the 1954 economic census. Soon there were much faster computers, and one called the 1105 was acquired by the

Census Bureau, along with additional university computers provided on a contract basis for the 1960 Census of Population and Housing.

In 1960 the population was 179.3 million. Other information gathered by the 159,000 enumerators resulted in a record 103,000 pages of published reports. Even with the electronic computer, however, the census took 1 million hours of preparation and cost almost $130 million. All respondents were asked name, address, relation to head of household, sex, color or race, month and year of birth, and marital status. Twenty-five percent were asked a more extensive list of questions.

Controversy returned, this time in the form of the great "data bank" threat. It was proposed for 1960 to use Social Security numbers as the key census identification for an individual's records. When Social Security numbers were first introduced, it had been promised that they would be confidential, and there was far greater protest over this threatened breach of confidentiality than had occurred over the "privy-toilet" question in 1940. The Bureau dropped the idea of putting Social Security numbers on census records.

A third generation of computers was available in the late 1960's, and the Bureau acquired the services of two 1107's and two 1108's for the 1970 census. These new machines came just in time. Their ability to read from magnetic tape at 150,000 characters a second helped census personnel keep up with the complexities of a more sophisticated census and an increasing population. The 1108 was 600 times as fast as the original UNIVAC.

The problem now was not so much the computer but the clumsiness of transferring hand-written data to a form the computer could process with its great speed. In the 1940's, the Bureau had contracted with computer firms for the design of such equipment, but none was completed in time for the 1950 census. Help was then requested from the U.S. Bureau of Standards, which in 1953 delivered what became known as FOSDIC, for Film Optical Sending Device for Input to Computers. Four production models of this optical scanner that converted penciled census forms into magnetic tape signals were used in the 1960 census and saved an estimated seven months of processing time.

## THE 1970 CENSUS

The population of the entire world in 1970 was estimated at about 3.6 billion, but in censuses of that year, taken in some ninety countries, only about half those humans were counted. This "people gap" existed because more than thirty countries have *never* taken a count of their people. Some, like China, have only estimates of their size, and China makes up almost a quarter of the world's population. On the other hand, some nations make a fetish of statistic gathering. In Japan, for example, schoolchildren enthusiastically urge parents to participate in the enumerations. In Ghana, church bells ring and sirens whine on census day; in Mexico one must be home when the census taker comes, or be fined $800.

Minsk-32 computers in the Soviet Union handled the job of processing data revealing that the population was 255 million. Surprisingly, the census also showed that more than half were not Russian but one of 109 other nationalities in the USSR. Other Communist countries taking censuses included Poland and Czechoslovakia.

United Nations census experts suggested standardized questionnaires and some progress was made. However, many differences persisted: Brazil asked about income but not color. Great Britain dropped income questions and added some on ethnic origins (because of growing immigrant communities). Communist countries elected not to include UN suggestions about religious preference; Russia classes "Jewish" as a nationality rather than a religion.

The 1970 United States census was the greatest effort yet taken. A total of 166,406 fairly well-paid enumerators counted 204.8 million Americans, and an office force of 4571 (down to less than half the number of the 1940 and 1950 efforts) converted 4 billion facts into some 200,000 pages of published reports. The cost of this effort was almost a quarter billion dollars; the cost per head counted was about $1.22, 122 times the per-capita cost of the 1790 effort.

For the first time since 1910 the Bureau used the mails for census questionnaires. This time it was "mail-out/mail-back," rather than the earlier one-way mail-back form. In most areas, response was extremely good from the 60 percent of the population who received these forms. Among them was Mary Beth Franzen, who probably wasn't aware that the grandmother she was named for had angrily tossed the first mail census forms into the trash sixty years before. To speed up data processing after the forms were in, an improved FOSDIC machine was produced. Processing 450 frames of microfilm a minute, it was four times as fast as the 1960 equipment, almost 2000 times as fast as punched-card techniques.

California gained 5 congressional seats, Florida three, and Arizona, Colorado, and Texas 1 each. New York and Pennsylvania each lost 2 seats, and Alabama, Iowa, North Dakota, Ohio, Tennessee, West Virginia, and Wisconsin lost 1 each, once again bearing out the importance of the original reason for the census.

A census of the deaf was taken in 1970, the first in forty years. There were 203 deaf persons for each 100,000 people, and a total of 13.4 million Americans had some hearing impairment. The rate of deaf to normal population was twice what it had been in 1930; such documentation was important to those funding aid for the deaf.

The 1970 census was first to give social and economic data on those of "Spanish origin" and Indians. More than 9 million of Spanish origin were counted, and 792,730 Indians. The census showed that farm population had declined by about one third in a decade. For the first time, more Americans lived in the suburbs than in the cities.

New York City lost more than 13,000 businesses between 1965 and 1970, Detroit lost 3500, and Philadelphia 3000. Those businesses didn't have to read the census figures for their own areas, but most likely they studied those for other parts of the country to find promising new locations. For example, XYZ Electronics on the outskirts of Philadelphia found that a small Georgia town had a large labor pool with sufficient skills for assembling the company's aircraft-crash-locator beacons. The town's tax policy for businesses was attractive too, and its climate would cut operating costs for the plant.

The Bureau admitted that it had missed a number of Americans in the census; estimates ranged from 4.8 to 5.8 million not counted, with a best estimate of 5.3 million (the total U.S. population in 1800). This error was just about 2.5 percent of the total, and perhaps as close as we can ever come in counting. Officials gave several reasons for the short count, including the resistance to census enumerators because of "increased alienation and distrust of authority," plus the reluctance of enumerators to work at night in some urban areas.

Resistance to census takers came from several types of people receiving questionnaires. The Joneses in Anaheim, California, had two draft-age sons and feared census returns might somehow make it more likely they would be called into service. Up in San Francisco, Mary Talbott (who took care of her four children with welfare money for dependent children) was not eager to list the children's father on a census form. And Tomas and Jesus Cruz in Phoenix were "wetbacks" who didn't want to be deported and so didn't answer the door of their shack when the census taker knocked.

## SUMMARY

In 190 years, many changes have taken place, both in the country itself and in the censuses that reflect the country. Population, the easiest characteristic to measure, exploded from 3.9 million to 203.2 million. Enumerators more than kept pace, climbing from 650 to 166,406, backed by a permanent office staff of 4,571. Total costs soared from the tiny $44,000 of the first effort in 1790 to almost $248 million in 1970; per-capita costs were up from 1.1 cents to about $1.22. But if census taking cost more, it produced more as well. In 1790, a modest 56 pages of published reports were the result; in 1970 the total was 200,000 pages, plus a wealth of data in other forms.

The Bureau itself had changed from an unskilled crew hastily put together from scratch every ten years to a respected army of career workers who have proved the Bureau's value many times over. Along the way it helped create the computer industry, data-users services that are revolutionizing government and business methods, and a Personal Services Department that supplies millions of Americans with information that can come only from the Census Bureau. The Bureau is indeed the number one "Fact Finder for the Nation."

# 3
# Fact Finder for the Nation

Probably no one who has not actually visited a Census Office in the
height of its work can form a conception of the extent and variety of the
materials which have there to be dealt with.

*Francis A. Walker*
*10th Superintendent of the Census*

The Bureau of the Census is a prestigious organization, properly
called "Fact Finder for the Nation." From year to year, the Bureau
collects information that forms a statistical mirror of our nation and
its people, linking generations and ages. Not just in America, but
throughout the world, it enjoys the reputation of being expert in
seeking out and publishing people-oriented and economic facts
useful to the many agencies and individuals who depend on such
information. The Bureau not only conducts regular censuses in
many fields, but carries out continuing related surveys. Thousands
of printed publications are produced each year, and information is
available in other forms as well, including computer tapes.

The Bureau of the Census is a vital agency, with an ensured and
growing future. It was not always so, however, and census historians have written of the rough and twisting road traversed by
determined administrators, statisticians, demographers, geogra-
phers, and others during the 190 years since the first United States
census in 1790.

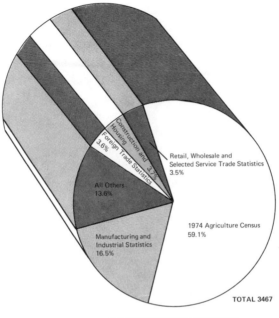

Retail, Wholesale and Selected Service Trade Statistics 3.5%

Construction and 3.7%

Housing

Foreign Trade Statistics 3.6%

All Others 13.6%

Manufacturing and Industrial Statistics 16.5%

1974 Agriculture Census 59.1%

TOTAL 3467

REPORTS PUBLISHED BY THE BUREAU
OF THE CENSUS IN FISCAL 1977

*The 1970 census resulted in reports useful to many different trades and services; this "pie" graph shows that nearly 60 percent of them were aimed at farming and allied businesses.*

## A LOOK AT THE CENSUS BUREAU

It was Moses who conducted the first biblical census, and America's census takers must have thought often of the wandering Jews as they moved from pillar to post in search of a home. Headquarters for the first census in 1790 was a building on New York's Broadway, on the east side of the street, so it can be said that "the Census opened on Broadway." Since that time all censuses have been conducted from the Washington, D.C., area, but at many different addresses.

61

In 1940, after 150 years of census taking, the Bureau finally had "permanent quarters" especially built for it on Virginia Avenue, S.W., between Second and Third Streets. But in 1942, because of pressures during wartime for office space in downtown Washington, it was forced out of its new home and moved to Suitland, Maryland. For the last 37 years the Bureau has remained there.

Suitland is a suburb of Washington, D.C., near Andrews Air Force Base. Amid rolling, tree-studded countryside, the town surrounds what is known as the Suitland Federal Center. Driving into the center one is greeted by an array of signs: Oceanographic to the left, Naval Intelligence, National Records Center, and Federal Buildings 3 and 4 to the right. There are *no* signs proclaiming the whereabouts of the Bureau of the Census, except on the two yellow-gray brick buildings themselves. Federal Buildings 3 and 4 have been compared to insurance company buildings, hospitals, warehouses, and even correctional institutions; at best, their modest outward appearance does not reflect the Bureau's importance.

The director and deputy director of the Census are assisted by the Data User Services Division, Public Information Program and Policy Development, and Equal Employment Opportunity Offices. Associate directors manage areas called Demographic Fields, Economic Fields, Statistical Standards and Methodology, Administration and Field Operations, and Information Technology. It will be explained later how these different areas affect the lives of individual citizens.

## THE CENSUS MISSION

In the beginning, Congress had to authorize each census with a special legislative act. Only in 1954 were census laws brought together under Title 13 of the United States Code, which outlines the basic scope of censuses and surveys, the obligation of the public to provide information, and the responsibility of the Bureau of the Census to keep that information confidential. Title 13 directs the Secretary of Commerce, through the Bureau of the Census, to take censuses of population, transportation, housing, agriculture, irrigation, drainage, and government at stated intervals. The Bureau of the Census may also take periodic surveys relevant to any of these subjects.

Bureau of the Census findings are used by the Congress, the executive branch, and the general public in the development and evaluation of social and economic programs. Among its many government "customers" are the Departments of Housing and Urban Development; Justice; Health, Education and Welfare; and Labor. The Bureau also uses information gathered by the various branches of government and by private organizations. Examples are the United Nations, the FBI, the Department of Agriculture, the Bureau of Mines, and the American Gas Association.

If Mr. Average Citizen were to meet and discuss the work of the Bureau with many of its experts in various fields, he might be grateful for the information received and for the keen interest and enthusiasm of the people. He would also be overwhelmed by the breadth and depth of the Bureau. One could spend months at the Bureau and barely scratch its surface. About 10,400 employees work for it full-time, and they are divided among several facilities. Some 2,800 are at headquarters in Suitland, Maryland, where one finds the Bureau's various divisions.

## DEMOGRAPHIC FIELDS

Demographic Fields, the "people" part of the Bureau, conducts censuses and surveys of population and housing. According to Daniel Levine, former Deputy Director for Demographic Fields, "People are the fulcrum. They are what it's all about here at the Bureau." He feels that the makeup of America has changed from its original melting-pot image to many separate groups. He considers us more a "confederation of minorities," not a homogeneous, constantly expanding glob of humanity but a mix of different kinds of people who act, react, and interact in so many different ways that it is very difficult to project or predict what our life-style will be in a few decades. For example, look at schools today; we have more than we need because Americans have cut back on having children.

A division of Demographic Fields is the International Statistical

Programs Center, a 145-member operation whose mission is to help foreign nations take useful censuses. This division has had Americans working in Saudi Arabia, Brazil, El Salvador, Bangladesh, Kenya, Pakistan, Bolivia, Costa Rica, the Dominican Republic, and the Philippines, to assist them in census taking.

Since 1946, the Center has trained more than 4,000 foreigners in census techniques. This work, done in more than ninety countries, forms a two-way program, because it also helps the United States gain accurate statistics on other nations. Indeed, ISPC maintains a file of population statistics from all over the world. The United Nations has recommended that all countries take censuses of population and housing in 1980, and ISPC is preparing training manuals to be used by some hundred developing nations which will participate.

The minority statistics program, which crosses several Bureau areas, includes the new Community Services Specialists, or CCS's. To aid minority groups, the Bureau hires these minority members CSS's, who live in the areas to be served. Much work is also being done with Indian tribes toward better mapping, so fewer people will be missed in censuses. Inadequate maps and indefinable boundaries on reservations are major problems, but there are others, including the fact that census questionnaires have stopped asking if a household has electricity, since it is assumed all do. Many Indian dwellings are still without such utilities, however.

## ECONOMIC FIELDS

Economic Fields conducts censuses and surveys covering Agriculture, Business, Construction, Foreign Trade, Governments, Mineral Industries, and Manufactures. This area has been quite successful in convincing business that the Bureau's efforts are worthwhile. There is still some complaint about the "response burden" of answering questionnaires, but most businessmen see the advantage in the information that results. At one point the Bureau decided to drop a survey of imports of gloves and mittens, but had to reinstate it quickly when letters and phone calls of protest poured in from buyers and others who relied heavily on the survey. The biggest problem is not with business, but with government administrators and bureaucrats, who occasionally try to cut back or even eliminate economic censuses or surveys.

## STATISTICAL STANDARDS AND METHODOLOGY

Statistical Standards and Methodology includes such far-out technologies as "remote-sensing" techniques for census work. Will we someday count people and houses with satellite photography? Maybe. In the 1980 census, testing is being done in thirty areas to compare "eye-in-the-sky" techniques with conventional census taking. Perhaps in 1990 this "remote sensing" will be more useful in census work.

## ADMINISTRATION

Besides administrative functions, this area includes Publications Services, Data Preparation, Geography, and Data User Services. The last of these rates special mention, and will be covered in detail in a later chapter.

## INFORMATION TECHNONOGY

A vital part of the Bureau is housed in its computer rooms. It was the Bureau of the Census that gave a start to the fledgling computer industry, and today an air-conditioned area in Building No. 3 houses some of the most sophisticated electronic data-processing equipment in the world. Working twenty-four hours a day—every day but Christmas!—the Bureau's computers and other equipment process billions of bits of information for censuses and surveys constantly being taken.

In the highly restricted computer section are banks of computers, tape readers, and printers that draw on a library of 120,000 reels of tape. In another large room, electronic printers spew out reams of data at hundreds of lines per minute.

The first step Bureau technicians take in changing our pencil-marked questionnaires into computer tapes is to photograph them. This is easier said than done with tens of millions of questionnaires to process, and the solution was a highly sophisticated machine that handles stacks of census forms, turns pages, and takes pictures of them. All this happens under strobe lights and takes place so fast it seems like magic. One machine turns sheets over so fast that the page simply seems to change by magic as you watch it.

There is even more magic in the Film Optical Sensing Device for Input to Computers, or FOSDIC machines. FOSDIC, envisioned and developed by the Bureau, is the electro-optical device that converts microfilm copies of questionnaires to magnetized bits of data on tapes. Tested first in the 1960 census, FOSDIC 70 starred in 1970. Working around the clock, 6 FOSDICS reduced 225 boxcar loads of forms to 14,000 tape reels containing 4 billion pieces of information! The scientific and technical competence of Bureau research and development groups is so high that the Bureau contracts research and development work for other agencies.

## THE CENSUS LIBRARY

Extensive library facilities are available at Suitland. More than 200,000 books and documents are available for general reference as well as detailed information on agriculture, business, construction, government, housing, industry, populations, statistical methodology, and electronic data processing. Special collections make the library unique. One of these includes all U.S. Census publications from 1790 to the present. A foreign and international collection contains statistical publications from most countries in the world. The library subscribes to some 1,200 periodicals. The principal reference collection includes documents from the fifty states, and from cities of more than 25,000 population, plus selected counties, towns, and special districts.

## THE MERCHANDISE

Although it is the decennial census that gets most attention, the Bureau does far more than count us all every ten years. Close to 2000 reports, surveys, and polls are published every year. These range from 2-page documents to others the size and scope of the *Statistical Abstract of the United States*, an information gold mine of a thousand pages that rivals the *World Almanac*. Much information is also available on magnetic tape for computer users.

Many newspaper headlines about population, education, employment (or unemployment), business, marriage, divorce, health, and accidents stem from Bureau of the Census surveys. The continuing Current Population Survey (CPS) is the largest conducted by the Bureau and requires interviews each month. Since there are 80 million or so households in the United States, and only 66,000 are sampled each month, great care must be taken so that those interviewed will accurately reflect the situation of the country as a whole. The odds are about 1500 to 1 that you have never had a CPS interviewer ring your doorbell or knock at the door, but that doesn't mean that someday one won't introduce herself (or himself) and start quizzing you on a variety of topics.

Conducted since 1940, CPS covers education, family size and migration, birth rates, income, and housing vacancies. From it comes information on the labor force, marital and family affairs, education, domestic help, occupational categories, and women in the work force. Current Population Surveys users include trade unions, vocational guidance counselors, and minority organizations to determine job opportunities in various places and for various kinds of people. Your school superintendent may rely on CPS for school enrollment projections, estimates of dropouts, nursery-school attendance, and other information. The manufacturer of that microwave oven you bought last week watches CPS data closely for sales potential in various market areas.

The Current Medicare Survey is a gauge of how well Medicare is working for you or your parents, and what changes should be made. This survey began in 1966, and today the Bureau interviews 7500 representative individuals each month. Is it working? Isn't it costing a lot more than anticipated? For business the Bureau conducts surveys including the Retail Trade Survey and Wholesale Trade Survey. There is even a Commercial Victimization Survey of crimes against business establishments. Your local supermarket manager may already have reported that break-in by thieves you heard about last month.

## FIELD OPERATIONS

Only about one in four Bureau people work in Suitland. Records processing and other clerical work is done in Jeffersonville, Indiana. More austere even than the Suitland facility, Jeffersonville resembles the former Army warehouse it used to be. The processing division is situated in Indiana because real estate is much cheaper and there is a ready pool of labor, much of it part-time, to accommodate the fluctuating work loads. Physical separation from Suitland is no problem, with electronic data links shuttling information almost instantly between the two facilities.

Farther west, in Pittsburg, Kansas, is the Bureau's Personal Census Service Branch, a little-known but very important operation. Though there is a rigid ban on releasing any personal information from census surveys, PCS breaks that rule in a very humane way. Any American (or his or her authorized representative in certain cases) can request proof of existence, age, citizenship, or family relationships. The fee is only a few dollars, and a typical search for such information usually takes only about two months.

That time your uncle needed proof of his age to qualify for admission to the retirement home, CPS could have saved his family time and money by checking old census records for the town where he was born. Keep that in mind if a need arises for that kind of information again.

Tens of thousands of information requests may be received in a single month, although they fluctuate seasonally and with such developments as Medicare and changes in Social Security regulations. More than 10 million citizens have been supplied with such needed information since 1935.

## REGIONAL CENSUS OFFICES

Suitland, Jeffersonville, and Pittsburg are the three focal points of census work, but to serve properly a nation of 220 million spread across fifty states, the Bureau also maintains a dozen regional offices. These outposts are sited in Atlanta; Boston; Charlotte,

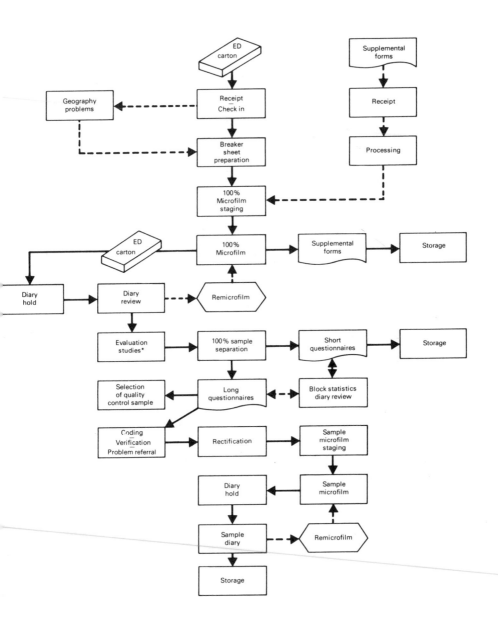

*A flow chart, showing how information is processed and stored by the modern Census Bureau.*

North Carolina; Chicago; Dallas; Denver; Detroit; Kansas City, Kansas; Los Angeles; New York; Philadelphia; and Seattle.

The Los Angeles Regional Office is at 11777 San Vicente Boulevard in Westwood. Offices are on the eighth floor, close to the Department of Commerce Business and Trade Offices. The mission of the Regional Office is two-fold: as an operational facility to carry out census and survey responsibilities, and as a Data User Services operation. About fifty people work for the Bureau at 11777 San Vincente; there are another three hundred elsewhere in the Los Angeles Region, which extends from Honolulu to Las Vegas.

A recent Los Angeles Office task was the selection of seventy workers for a special political survey for the State of California. Complicating the effort was the passage of Proposition 13 and the subsequent tightening of money available to state agencies. Another special survey was done of elections in California. The state and the federal government are interested in seeing what results have come of the strong civil-rights measures of the last several years. Are minority voters turning out for elections, or are there still problems of this nature? With survey findings, government agencies can plan necessary follow-up.

Regional offices are important in another way too. Should you be interested in working for the Census Bureau, keep in mind that in addition to hiring workers for the Current Population Surveys and other ongoing efforts, the Los Angeles Office alone used some 30,000 workers in the field for the 1980 census.

Many states have no regional office; Arizona, for example, is served by the regional office in Denver, Colorado. From that office the most frequent visitor to Arizona is the Data User Services officer who makes regular trips around the region, heading up workshops and seminars for users and potential users of Census data.

## CAREERS WITH THE CENSUS

If you are interested in working for the Bureau of the Census, there are two ways to go about it. The simpler one is to get a temporary job as an interviewer or enumerator. Thousands work on a "regular part-time" basis for the Current Population Survey; several hundred thousand work for a few weeks or months every ten years (that may change to every five years with the introduction of the 5-year census in 1985). A deeper commitment would be to join the Bureau as a career employee.

For many, work with the Bureau of the Census is an entry into the field of government or business, a way of acquiring experience and skill in areas much in demand elsewhere. However, the arrow can point in the other direction too, and some Bureau employees come from related fields in other governmental agencies, or in business.

The Census Bureau employs statisticians, economists, demographers, and sociologists. There are also opportunities for those with training in electronic data processing. Administrative divisions offer jobs to those with business administration, public administration, social science, or liberal arts backgrounds. The Bureau strongly encourages advanced study, and financial assistance for employees is available under various plans for work in colleges and universities. In-service training is provided in computer science and managerial development, and informal training is common in other specialized fields. Hundreds of Census Bureau employees attend college courses or are involved in governmental interagency programs. Bureau employees have memberships in more than two dozen professional organizations.

Some foreign assignments are available for career employees, usually for 2-year periods, in support of Census programs in foreign nations. These assignments are in population studies, economics, and data processing, and usually are offered only after three to five years experience.

For a copy of "Professional Careers in Census," or other employment information, write to:

U.S. Bureau of the Census
Personnel Division
College Relations Office
Washington, D.C.

## THE BUREAU'S FUTURE

Any organization doing as much as the Bureau of the Census does cannot please everyone all the time. There is an old joke about the man who sarcastically suggested that all census workers be fired and the information garnered from the *World Almanac*. Serious critics of the Bureau still suggest that the Bureau does get much information elsewhere, thus duplicating expensive services. Some charge that too *much* information is released; others fault the Bureau for not releasing enough information sooner. A former Bureau employee has charged that late reporting in some surveys led to the 1973–1974 recession.

E. J. Kahn, author of *The American People*, comments that "the Census Bureau's scrupulous devotion to anonymity obliges it to leave in its statistically churning wake all sorts of teasing flotsam." Among such riddles he mentions 1970 census statistics to the effect that 249 of the nation's blacksmiths were women, of whom 6 were working in eating and drinking places and 11 in credit agencies, hardly likely places for female iron benders. Kahn also pointed to census data on doctors, which indicated they employed 11 airline hostesses, 7 railroad switchmen, 39 physicists and astronomers, and 4 female fishermen.

With all its faults—and Bureau officials admit to them—the future of the Census seems ensured. While some people can't get along with it, America as a whole can't get along without it. The Bureau, wherever it gets its statistics, publishes the bulk of the nation's informational documents and in most cases, when the government needs statistics, the Bureau is asked to provide them. Business, too, relies very strongly on the Census Bureau. There is little question that the Bureau will survive and grow. Not only will it continue to mirror what happens in the future, it will increasingly affect us as we apply Lincoln's homely yardstick of knowing where we are so we can better plan where we are going.

# 4
# Mirror of the People

And so it happens that the United States alone among nations possesses a complete comparative record of population, from the date when the independent nation was born.

S. N. D. North, Director
Bureau of the Census (1903–1909)

The census has been called a "portrait of the people," but this falls short of an accurate description. Rather than portraits, the ongoing censuses and surveys are a *continuous reflection* of the American people and of their actions: a mirror of our lives and times.

Humorists point out that the average American male is 89 percent white, 44.2 years old, with a wife 41.3, each of them having 12.3 years of education. They have 2.35 children, drive 1.4 automobiles, own 1.5 TV sets, and live in a house with 5.3 rooms worth approximately $49,000. Such averages are useful at times, but the fact is that America is made up of 220 million *individuals* in all shapes and sizes, several colors, and a broad range of preferences, abilities, and achievements. The melting pot has not homogenized us all that much.

Censuses once counted only males who were heads of households, or old enough to go to war. Anyone wanting to know the number of women and children and other statistics had to do it by

73

guesswork. That is no longer the case, for the census has been counting people in dozens of specific categories for decades. How many women are there in each age bracket? How many children under 16 years, or under 6 months? How many males over 65, or under 18? How many deaf people, how many of Spanish origin? What is the average, median, or whatever other index one wants?

The following randomly selected news stories give an idea of the range of information periodically reported by the Bureau of the Census:

About 86 percent of Americans drive cars to work.

Three houses in four are insulated.

Only one couple in five lives to celebrate a fiftieth wedding anniversary; two marriages in five end in divorce, but four of five divorced persons remarry.

Counties spend $6 billion on education, and $7 billion on welfare.

The biggest gripe in the country in 1976 was noise, with 49.2 percent of those polled thinking their environment was too noisy.

In 1968, 77 percent of eligible voters were registered for the presidential election. By 1976 only 66.7 were registered.

Prices of private houses in 1977 averaged $54,000; homeowners had a median income of $21,000, renters only $10,792.

From World War I to 1974, the number of horses and mules on American farms decreased from 25 million to 3 million; tractors were up from 250,000 to 5 million.

The United States spent $10.2 billion on pollution control in 1976.

In 1975 there were 5,318,000 Boy Scouts and 3,234,000 Girl Scouts in the United States.

## AN AMERICAN PROFILE

It is population that generally comes to mind first when we think of the census. Size is important; we tend to equate bigness with goodness, and want our city, state, or nation to be the biggest regardless of the problems that come with size. Certainly our nation has grown dramatically in its first two centuries; our numbers have increased until there are 55 times as many as were counted in 1790.

It might be suspected that those paid to count population would be tempted to claim more people than there really are. Many "ghosts" have voted, for example. However, the Census Bureau has never counted all Americans, and more than 5 million were missed during the 1970 census. Among the missing are illegal aliens, but minority organizations have charged that the Bureau of the Census also misses many blacks, elderly, and Spanish-speaking citizens. Surely it is the minorities, the old folks, and those who do not speak the language who are most likely to be missed in the census. Because this affects welfare and other social services, the Bureau is constantly attempting to improve methods so that fewer will be missed each year.

On January 1, 1978, America's population (including our armed forces overseas) was estimated by the Bureau at 217,874,000. This was 1,836,000 more than the year before. Of the total population, 24.5 million were blacks. People of Spanish origin totaled about 11.3 million, including Mexican, Puerto Rican, Cuban, Central and South Americans, and others.

There were 6.4 million fewer American children under 14 than in 1970 because of the decline in the birth rate, or only 1.8 children per woman during her lifetime. The population between 25 and 34 years increased by 32 percent, and for those older than 65 it went up 18 percent. As a result of these shifts, the median age of America increased from 27.9 years in 1970 to 29.4 in 1977.

Although the total population increased between 1970 and 1977, some age groups *lost* population because of the declining birth rate. For example, there were 1.9 million fewer children under 4 years of age, and 4.4 million fewer in the 5–13 bracket. On the other hand, there were 8 million more in the 25–34 bracket, and 3.5 million more in the over-65 bracket. There were 6.5 percent more women, compared with only 5.7 percent more men. This reflects the fact that women as a group survive longer than men.

The white population in the central cities dropped 8 percent since 1970; the black population increased by 6 percent. The move to the suburbs continued, and the sun-belt states of California, Florida, and Texas accounted for 40 percent of the 13 million in population growth.

75

## OLDER MEN PER 1000 OLDER WOMEN

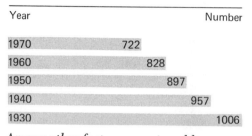

| Year | Number |
|------|--------|
| 1970 | 722 |
| 1960 | 828 |
| 1950 | 897 |
| 1940 | 957 |
| 1930 | 1006 |

*Among other facts concerning old age, recent censuses have revealed by what increasing numbers women are outliving men.*

A dramatic change was found among young women. In 1960, 28 percent of women between 20 and 24 were single; by 1977, 45 percent in that bracket were single! More women between 25 and 29 also delayed marriage. In 1977 there were an estimated 8.1 million divorced men and women who had not remarried. In 1960 there had been only 35 divorced persons for each 1,000 married persons; by 1977 there were 84. It is interesting to note that the probability of divorce decreases with education. College graduates account for only 29 percent of divorced women, whereas those who have not completed college will record 49 percent divorces.

Nearly a million unmarried couples were living together in 1977, almost double the figure for 1970. In 1978 there were 76 million households in the United States, three of four consisting of families. Of nonfamily households, seven out of eight were persons living alone. This increasing number of one-person households, or of two adults with no children, has brought the average number per household from 3.14 in 1970 down to 2.86 in 1977.

*In the last nine decades family size has slowly but inexorably decreased; census figures show that the 1970 family averaged only slightly over three persons.*

### AVERAGE SIZE OF HOUSEHOLD: 1890-1970

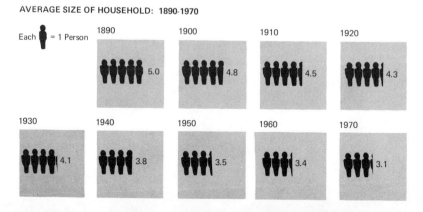

The American life-style is changing, in some areas drastically. Statistics that reflect these changes are important, not just to those who make the statistics, but to governments, educators, builders, the sellers of food and goods, insurance companies—the whole range of American government and business. These statistics are also important to the individuals who create them.

Looking in the census mirror, we see changes in a great number of Americans but what is more important, we see changes in the relative numbers of young and old. With fewer young people and more old people, we seem to be heading for a more mature America instead of one dominated by the young. This change is having its effect on schools and on teachers, who no longer have an easy time getting and keeping jobs.

An even stronger force than age is at work. This is the change in values for young women, who obviously now put more emphasis on careers than on marriage and children. With or without the passage of the Equal Rights Amendment, women have emancipated themselves from housewifery and child bearing. This will have more effect on the American way of life than just giving men more competition for jobs. It will continue the trend toward fewer births during a woman's lifetime, thus edging us toward the Zero Population Growth cherished by many. And it will result in more one-person households.

The emancipated American woman also participates in more unmarried partnership arrangements. Our morals, our ethics, and our religious values plainly are undergoing revolutionary changes. The changes affect the environment in which children are growing up, and future censuses will record the results.

## ETHNIC GROUPS

Nearly half of our forefathers came from Great Britain and Ireland. Most of the others came from Germany, Italy, Poland, Russia, and other European countries, such as Austria, Czechoslovakia, France, The Netherlands, Norway, and Sweden.

In 1970 there were 178 million white Americans, 22.5 million blacks, 793,000 Indians, 591,000 Japanese, 435,000 Chinese,

293,000 Filipinos, and 593,000 of other races. Except for American Indians, all Americans are immigrants or the descendants of immigrants. And the Indians themselves came into the country from Asia, making us *all* immigrants! Indeed, our traditional image has been that of a great melting pot of humanity mostly funneled into America through the tiny immigration station at Ellis Island in New York Harbor. The purpose of the Statue of Liberty was immortalized in verse by Emma Lazarus:

> Give me your tired, your poor,
> Your huddled masses yearning to breathe free,
> The wretched refuse of your teeming shore,
> Send these, the homeless, tempest-tossed to me.
> I lift my lamp beside the golden door!

These words were set down almost a century ago, but they still apply. Consider the tragic "boat people" fleeing Viet Nam and finding a haven in that same America that Emma, herself of an uprooted minority fleeing Russia, praised in her poem "The New Colossus."

For years there were few restrictions on immigration into America, and from 1820 to 1970 about 50 million foreigners came here. In the one decade from 1901 to 1910 almost 9 million immigrants arrived. There had been a few laws passed by Congress to keep out aliens; a separate law was passed in 1882 at the insistence of American labor to exclude the Chinese because they were working for low wages and taking work from Americans. But in 1921 Congress set restrictive quotas for immigrants from outside the Western Hemisphere, and this resulted in an appreciable reduction in immigration. Legislation in 1965 abolished national quotas, but kept an overall limitation on the number of immigrants. Today, about 300,000 foreigners a year come into America. Ellis Island ceased to function as the entry point for foreign newcomers in the 1950's, and immigrants now arrive at all regular ports of entry.

In 1970 there were 9.6 million legal foreign-born Americans. Additional numbers cross our borders illegally. California and New York are home for more than 40 percent of the foreign-born, with

Native of Foreign or Mixed Parentage

Foreign Born

EACH SYMBOL=250,000 PERSONS

| United Kingdom | 1,778,951 |
| | 686,099 |
| Ireland | 1,198,845 |
| | 251,375 |
| Germany | 2,789,070 |
| | 832,965 |
| Poland | 1,826,137 |
| | 548,107 |
| U.S.S.R. | 1,479,733 |
| | 463,462 |
| Italy | 3,232,246 |
| | 1,008,533 |
| Other Europe | 5,535,854 |
| | 1,921,485 |
| Asia | 920,475 |
| | 824,887 |
| Canada | 2,222,135 |
| | 812,421 |
| Mexico | 1,579,440 |
| | 759,711 |

MOTHER TONGUE BY NATIVITY: 1970

Native

Foreign Born

EACH SYMBOL=5 PERCENT

| English | 86.3% |
| | 17.8% |
| French | 1.2% |
| | 4.3% |
| German | 2.7% |
| | 12.6% |
| Polish | 1.1% |
| | 4.4% |
| Russian | 0.1% |
| | 1.6% |
| Yiddish | 0.6% |
| | 4.6% |
| Italian | 1.7% |
| | 10.8% |
| Spanish | 3.3% |
| | 17.8% |
| All Other | 3.1% |
| | 26.1% |

*Two graphs from the 1970 census show that, although 86.3 percent of us are native speakers of English, we still have a large population of foreign-born or second-generation Americans.*

Europeans settling in New York and Asians in California. Canadians tend to settle in states along our northern border, and those from Mexico and other Latin-American countries largely in the South and West. Florida, for example, is the adopted home of many refugees from Cuba.

The foreign-born have had only 7.4 years of schooling, against 12.1 for all Americans. However, their median income in 1970 was $9,026, compared with $9,590 for all Americans. The foreign-born had a median age of 52.0 years, compared with 28.1 for all Americans.

## ASIAN-AMERICANS

Our Asian-Americans are becoming a force to be reckoned with. Their population increased by 55 percent from 1960 to 1970, whereas total population went up only 13.3 percent. The 520,000 Asian-Americans who live in California make up only 2.6 percent of the population, but the 373,000 in Hawaii represent nearly half that state's total. Chinese-Americans account for most of the Asian population elsewhere in America.

Living mostly in urban areas and holding good jobs, Asian-Americans have high incomes. In fact, the Japanese-American median in 1970 was $12,515, almost $3000 higher than that for the nation. The Chinese-Americans had a median income of $10,610, also above the national figure. Filipino-Americans earned $9,318, just under the national figure. Eager for schooling, Asian-Americans are far above the national figures for college work; 26 percent of Chinese-Americans over 25 years of age have completed four years of college. For Americans as a whole, only 11 percent have done so.

## BLACKS

In 1978 there were 24.5 million black people, up almost 2 million since the 1970 census, and now more than Canada's total population. They still represent only 11 percent of the population of the United States, however, no more than they did as far back as 1900. The percentage has actually dropped since the first census in 1790, when the 760,000 blacks were about 20 percent of the total. However, black people are still our largest minority, and estimates that perhaps six times as many blacks as whites are missed in the census indicate an even higher black population. Black people average several years younger than whites, with a median age of 21.0 for males and 23.6 for females.

Great progress in black employment is reflected in census figures. Some 7.3 million were employed; 3.3 million of them women. In 1960 there were only 280,000 black professionals; by 1970 that had increased to 611,000. Black engineers had jumped from 312 in 1960 to 13,000 in 1970. Female black secretaries increased from 21,000 in 1960 to 88,000 in 1970, with a drop in household workers from 888,000 to 509,000. Encouraging as these statistics were, another was not so bright: the median income for blacks was only $6,279, much less than that for the total population.

# INDIANS

It is ironic that the Indians, who were the first Americans, are today the smallest ethnic group in the nation. However, in 1970 there were 792,730 Indians in America, an increase of 51 percent over 1960 and a much greater increase than for the nation as a whole. Their median age was 20.4 years, compared to the national median of 29.4, because the life expectancy of Indians is much shorter than average.

Indians were not counted on a regular basis in the census until 1930, and only with the 1960 census did self-identification become the basis for the count.

The largest Indian tribes in 1970 were:

| | |
|---|---|
| Navajo | 96,743 |
| Cherokee | 66,150 |
| Sioux | 47,825 |
| Chippewa | 41,946 |
| Lumbee | 27,520 |
| Choctaw and Houma | 23,562 |
| Apache | 22,993 |
| Iroquois | 21,473 |
| Creek, Alabama, and Coushatta | 17,004 |

About half the Indians live in rural areas, more than a quarter on major reservations, and the rest on small reservations or in urban areas. Nearly half the Indian population is concentrated in the West, a fourth in the South, nearly a fifth in the North Central, and the remaining 5 percent or so in the Northeast.

Perhaps because so many Indians cling to reservation life, the median family income in 1970 was only $5,832, about 60 percent of the national average. Nearly 40 percent of Indians were living below the poverty level; in Tucson, Arizona, about 60 percent were in this category.

Although most Indians work, their unemployment rate is about three times the national average. Their educational status is improving, however, with about 33 percent of those over 25 having completed high school. More than half the Indians between the ages of 3 and 34 were in school, including 95 percent of those between 7 and 13. College enrollment has doubled since 1960. Median years of schooling for Indians was 9.8, about the same as for blacks.

Though it is true that Indians tend to stay with the old culture of the tribe and live on the reservation, census statistics tell a surprising story about Indians and marriage.

More than a third of Indians marry non-Indians. This is remarkably higher than the 0.7 percent for other ethnic groups who cross lines in marriages. If the trend continues, it could conceivably lead to the gradual disappearance of Indians as an ethnic group.

## SPANISH ORIGINS

In 1970, questions were added to the census forms to clarify the status of Spanish-Americans. One new question read: "Is this person's origin or descent Mexican, Puerto Rican, Cuban, Central or South American, other Spanish, or none of these?" Of the 12 million Spanish-speaking people in America in 1978, 7.2 million were of Mexican origin, 1.8 million Puerto Rican, 700,000 Cuban, 900,000 Central or South American, and 1.5 million of other Spanish origin.

About 2.9 million Spanish-origin people were employed in America in 1970, slightly more than one third of them women. Proportionately fewer women of this minority group are working than among blacks and whites. This reflects a cultural pattern of women staying in the home. Males were predominantly in skilled blue-collar jobs, service occupations, and professional and technical jobs. Women worked at clerical jobs, as operatives, and in service occupations, with secretarial work most popular.

For men, the median income was $7,797, compared to the national median of $10,261. Spanish-origin women did better, with incomes of $3,669, compared to the national median for women of $3,956. This was because about half the employed women held white-collar jobs; only about one quarter of the men did. About 85 percent of those of Spanish origin live in metropolitan areas, compared with 65 percent for all families. The 21 percent living below the poverty level were more than double the national average. Like other minority groups in America, Spanish-origin people are young, with a median age of only 21 in 1970.

An interesting ethnic census statistic is the fact that for each 100 white women there are 97.3 men. For each 100 black women, there are only 93.3 men and the Japanese ratio is 91.6 men per 100 women. But for Indians the ratio swings the other way, with 101.1 men to 100 women. Chinese males predominate by 139.4 to 100, and Filipinos by the great margin of 172.4 to 100. The top-heavy numbers of male Chinese and Filipinos result from immigration laws that admitted far more males than females.

## RELIGION

Biblical censuses counted only people of the Jewish faith; early French censuses, only those who were Catholic, the state religion. Today the Bureau takes no religious censuses, but it can give population estimates of the many religions in the United States. From 1850 to 1890 the Census Office gathered information on churches, membership, value of church structures, and other information in special surveys during the Censuses of Population. Between 1905 and 1936, several Censuses of Religious Bodies were taken. Because of some objections to such censuses, no more have been taken, and information is now gathered by the Bureau of the Census from religious organizations. However, in 1957, the Bureau did conduct a sample survey, asking, "What is your religion?" on a voluntary basis. Although it is generally thought that most Americans are white Anglo-Saxon Protestants, only about 30 percent are in this category. This does not make them a minority, however, for there is no other larger group. About 26 percent of Americans are Catholics; only 3 percent are Jewish.

Concern is often expressed that religious faith is dying in America, but statistics do not bear this out. In 1975, for example, 332,465 churches were reported, with a combined membership of more than 132 million, almost two thirds of the population. Protestants numbered 72,485,000, Catholics 48,702,000, and Jews 3,696,000. Only a little over 3.1 million reported no religious affiliation.

Private survey figures also disclose that it is not Catholics but Baptists who are most prolific; when Protestants are taken altogether, their birth rate about matches that of Catholics. Jews have a birth rate about 25 percent lower than either Protestants or Catholics. Of all married couples, 94 percent of spouses are of the same religion. In the 6 percent of mixed marriages (with respect to religion), most are Catholics (2.2 percent marry out of their faith), followed by Protestants, and then Jews, who cling most closely to tradition. There is also a correlation between religion and income, with Jews earning most, followed by Catholics, and finally Protestants.

## EDUCATION

In 1977 there were about 60 million students between the ages of 3 and 34 in American schools. Another 1.3 million over 35 were in colleges or universities. About one student in eight attended a private school. Costs for education were about $120 billion, roughly 7.5 percent of the GNP.

Illiteracy was present in only about 2.2 percent of the population. For whites the rate was only 1.6 percent; blacks had a 7.5 percent illiteracy rate. One in four whites and one in nine blacks completed college. Overall, about 65 percent of the population 25 and older had graduated from high school, up from only 55 percent in 1970. Only in kindergarten were enrollments down—because of the declining birth rate.

There were more than 79,000 elementary schools (14,000 of them private); 29,500 secondary schools (3,600 private); and more than 2,700 colleges and universities (1,520 private). Staffing the schools were about 2,400,000 elementary and secondary teachers, and 640,000 college and university instructors. For those who couldn't get enough information in school, there were 30,436 libraries in the United States.

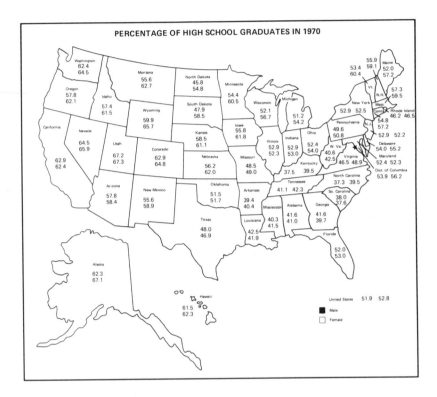

PERCENTAGE OF HIGH SCHOOL GRADUATES IN 1970

*Recent census reports show percentages of high-school graduates by states; Utah leads the nation with 67.2 percent of males and 67.3 percent of females.*

## AMERICANS AT WORK

It is puzzling that in a society of "labor-saving" devices and constantly increasing productivity, more instead of fewer of us are working. Most of the increase involves women. In 1977 the United States labor force, including the armed forces, climbed past 100 million for the first time. Women accounted for 41 percent of that total, and for 57 percent of the increase since 1970, demonstrating how rapidly women are getting into career fields. Of all married women, 46 percent were working. And of nearly 8 million female heads of households, 56 percent were at work.

Unemployment was about 7 percent overall. However, there were soft spots in such fields as entertainment and recreation (11.4 percent) and construction (10.3 percent). Unemployment for blacks and other minorities ended the year at 13.3 percent, nearly double that for the nation as a whole, and about the same as the previous year. In both 1976 and 1977, minority teenagers had the highest unemployment rate of any segment, at 40.8 percent in July of 1977.

Even within the Bureau of the Census, it should be noted, there is debate as to just what constitutes unemployment. Decades ago, when women were a small minority in the work force, there were perhaps as large a percentage out of work as there are today. How many Americans *should* be working, and by what age? Tables show many 16-year-olds "unemployed," and a Census Bureau professional noted that many adults claiming to be unemployed are "80 years old and suffering a terminal disease."

The 1820 census recorded only three categories of employment: farming, manufacturing, and commerce. The 1970 census reported more than 25,000 different occupations. Fortunately, most of these can be grouped together under the dozen major headings used by the Bureau of the Census. Here is where Americans worked in 1970:

| Occupation Group | Number Employed |
|---|---|
| Clerical | 13.7 million |
| Professional and technical | 11.4 million |
| Craftsmen | 10.6 million |
| Operatives, except transport | 10.5 million |
| Service workers, except household | 8.6 million |
| Managers and administrators except farm | 6.4 million |
| Sales | 5.4 million |
| Laborers, except farm | 3.4 million |
| Transport equipment | 3.0 million |
| Farmers and farm managers | 1.4 million |
| Private households | 1.1 million |
| Farm laborers and foremen | 0.9 million |

MAJOR OCCUPATION OF EMPLOYED PERSONS By Race and Sex: 1970 and 1960

| | | WHITE: Male | Female | NEGRO AND OTHER RACES: Male | Female |
|---|---|---|---|---|---|

Data relate to persons
14 years old and over

EACH SYMBOL=500,000 PERSONS
NUMBERS IN THOUSANDS

| Occupation | Year | White Male | Negro and Other Races: Male | White Female | Negro and Other Races: Female |
|---|---|---|---|---|---|
| Professional, Technical and Kindred Workers | 1970 | 6,198.7 | 317.9 | 3,907.5 | 406.6 |
| | 1960 | 4,158.6 | 144.6 | 2,485.3 | 197.4 |
| Managers and Administrators, except Farm | 1970 | 4,971.7 | 153.8 | 958.3 | 55.5 |
| | 1960 | 4,696.1 | 100.7 | 795.2 | 33.8 |
| Sales Workers | 1970 | 3,171.1 | 96.6 | 1,909.2 | 90.6 |
| | 1960 | 2,925.2 | 60.7 | 1,606.0 | 45.5 |
| Clerical and Kindred Workers | 1970 | 3,116.4 | 335.8 | 8,863.4 | 719.0 |
| | 1960 | 2,723.1 | 198.8 | 5,984.7 | 219.1 |
| Craftsmen and Kindred Workers | 1970 | 8,879.3 | 622.3 | 446.2 | 48.7 |
| | 1960 | 8,239.4 | 428.3 | 256.4 | 20.7 |
| Operatives, except Transport | 1970 | 5,339.4 | 756.9 | 3,193.8 | 526.1 |
| | 1960 | 5,112.9 | 573.9 | 2,819.5 | 315.9 |
| Transport Equipment Operatives | 1970 | 2,264.4 | 379.9 | 109.0 | 12.8 |
| | 1960 | 2,164.6 | 323.5 | 34.4 | 3.5 |
| Laborers, except Farm | 1970 | 2,345.4 | 599.3 | 220.5 | 48.1 |
| | 1960 | 2,365.9 | 783.2 | 136.2 | 36.5 |
| Farmers and Farm Managers | 1970 | 1,243.5 | 37.7 | 58.6 | 3.3 |
| | 1960 | 2,213.4 | 176.0 | 100.7 | 17.2 |
| Farm Laborers and Farm Foremen | 1970 | 637.7 | 145.4 | 108.9 | 31.8 |
| | 1960 | 947.5 | 291.1 | 171.3 | 76.3 |
| Service Workers, except Private Household | 1970 | 3,008.1 | 632.3 | 3,612.5 | 811.6 |
| | 1960 | 2,231.4 | 560.0 | 2,415.2 | 547.7 |
| Private Household Workers | 1970 | 22.2 | 17.4 | 533.2 | 519.9 |
| | 1960 | 31.6 | 29.5 | 758.4 | 898.4 |

NOTE: Persons with occupation not reported are excluded.

1970 CENSUS OF POPULATION, U.S. Department of Commerce, Social and Economic Statistics Administration, Bureau of the Census

*Who holds what kind of job? Facts gathered from the 1960 and 1970 censuses show numbers employed in various trades, black employment compared with white. Such figures help strengthen campaigns to equalize employment practices.*

87

Of less than 4 million Americans in 1790, there were 2.1 million farming. Of the 203 million Americans in 1970, there were still only 2.3 million. So there must be many new kinds of jobs today. In 1970 there were 255,000 computer specialists and 80,000 operations analysts counted. As these occupations were added, others were dropped, such as baby-sitters. Also, with more time and money available, employment in the creative professions grew to more than 750,000. Athletes, enjoying great popularity and even greater salaries, numbered 35,000 men and 14,000 women, far more than the 5,900 actors and 3,900 actresses. There were 18,000 men and 7,000 women authors. Women dancers outnumbered men 5,000 to 1,100, but men led in all other creative occupations, particularly as radio and television announcers. Of these, 20,000 were men and only 1,500 women, although a woman named Barbara Walters was earning a million dollars a year.

As more women enter the world of work, more older people retire. The employment rate for men 55–64 dropped from 83 percent in 1970 to only 74 percent employed in 1977. Better retirement plans plus increasing competition from women seem to be among the reasons for earlier male retirement.

In 1975 weekly earnings for full-time wage and salary personnel averaged $185, or $55 more than in 1970. However, expressed in "constant dollars" adjusted for inflation and other factors, 1975 earnings were only $116, compared with $112 in 1970. So if you have the feeling you are trying to go up on the down escalator it is understandable. It is interesting to compare average weekly wages and salaries with some union pay scales for skilled workers. By 1975, such scales had risen in some locations to $10 an hour and more in some jobs. Journeymen in Dallas earned $8.00 an hour, in Philadelphia they earned $10.27 for the same work. Such incomes rival those of many professionals.

Median family income, in constant dollars, had *declined* in 1974 and again in 1975. In 1976 it increased to $14,960. White families had a median income of $15,540, those of Spanish origin, $10,260, and black families, $9,240. Families with no husband present had a median income of only $7,210. The difference between median incomes of men and women was still very great, with $9,430 for men and $3,580 for women.

About 25 million Americans in 1976 had incomes below the poverty level, set at $5,815 for a nonfarm family of four and adjusted for other situations. The percentage of people below the poverty level was not significantly different from that of 1969. Blacks and other minorities, the elderly, and families headed by women made up a large share of the poor. Of the 25 million poor in 1976, blacks accounted for 30 percent, people of Spanish origin for 11 percent, the elderly (those over 65) for 13 percent, and female householder families for 36 percent.

## AMERICANS ON THE MOVE

The census keeps tab on the movement of our people as they play out their game of musical chairs. Some researchers claim it was John Babson Lane Soule, and not Horace Greeley, who first said, "Go west, young man." Whoever said it, Americans have heeded that advice. We are historically a westward-moving people; the great western movement of pioneer days and the 1849 gold rush added large numbers to our western states. There have been other exoduses such as that of "Okies" and "Arkies" fleeing the harsh life of the Dust Bowl in the 1930's. More Americans once lived in the East and the North, but recently the population scales have tipped, and for the first time more of us are living in the South and West.

One obvious reason for the relative ease with which Americans move about is the fact that we are a nation on wheels. In 1913, there were only 1 million cars in America. By 1975 there were 107 million, plus 26 million trucks and buses. About 39 percent of households had one car; more than 45 percent had two or more. In 1975, only a little over 50 percent of the population had remained in the same house since 1970. Nearly 25 percent had moved to a different house in the same county. About 17 percent had moved to another county, and almost 9 percent to another state. It is interesting to note that those who moved most were those earning the least.

Much human movement is puzzling. For example, in a year when almost a million Americans moved from farms, another 440,000 moved *to* farms! And whereas 33,000 Nebraskans moved to California, more than 9,000 moved from California to Nebraska.

The net farm exodus is real, however, and each year a sizable percentage of the population pulls up its roots in rural areas and replants them in cities or suburbs.

We hear a great deal about the pull of the "big city," but more than 70 percent of us live in cities smaller than 100,000. Only about 16 percent live in cities of over half a million. Perhaps there is a maximum survival size for cities, as our largest seem to be in deep trouble. New York City has lost population in the last several censuses, and so have Philadelphia, Detroit, Chicago, Boston, Buffalo, and Akron.

If farms are losing population, and likewise some large cities, there must be balancing growth in other areas. Those areas are the suburbs. The preferred life-style for increasing numbers of Americans is residence not in but *near* a large city. This "best of both worlds" means the attractions of a city close at hand, and the benefits of a less hectic life around home. Statisticians point out that it is easy to understand the appeal of the suburbs: suburban resi-

*Where America's 2,314,013 farms are concentrated—facts gathered from enumerations on the 1970s.*

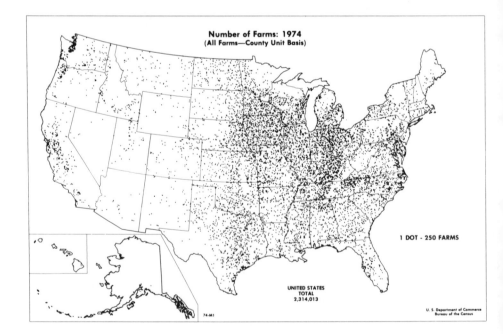

Number of Farms: 1974
(All Farms—County Unit Basis)

1 DOT - 250 FARMS

UNITED STATES
TOTAL
2,314,013

74-M1

U. S. Department of Commerce
Bureau of the Census

*The Census of Agriculture, though not as well known as the population count, is of vital importance to farmers and ranchers everywhere.*

dents are richer ($7,114 in 1960, compared with $5,945 for city dwellers and only $3,228 for farm families); unemployment is less than in the cities; suburbanites tend to be professionals, to own their homes, to have more rooms (including bathrooms) in those homes, and to be younger. An earlier book on the census evaluated all the data and humorously advised anyone wanting to be prosperous in America to be a white doctor with a private practice, to live in the suburbs of a western city, have a working wife and three children, and be a veteran between the ages of 45 and 49!

In 1975, Arizona led the nation in population gain with 4.4 percent for the year. Right behind were Florida, at 4.1 percent, Nevada, 3.7 percent, and Alaska, 3.0 percent. California gained only 1.1 percent, but since the state was already huge, the additional numbers involved were greater than in states with higher percentage gains. But while some areas grew, others shrank. New

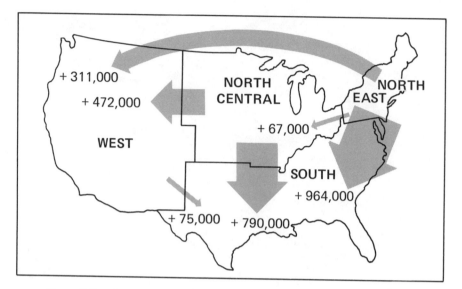

+ 311,000
+ 472,000
WEST
NORTH CENTRAL
NORTH EAST
+ 67,000
SOUTH
+ 964,000
+ 75,000    + 790,000

*One of the Census Bureau's most important services is charting of population redistribution, to determine Congressonal representation. As shown here, people have been leaving the North and East and moving to the South and West.*

York State gained population, for instance, but New York City lost some. With population generally rising at about 10 percent per decade, a state that shows a loss between censuses is losing indeed.

Americans are moving away from the rural South, away from farmland in the middle of the country, away from the impoverished Ozarks and Appalachia, and also away from the industrialized East. There are numerous examples of such regions losing population for economic reasons as residents leave to seek brighter futures in states that are booming. More surprising are the losses from such northeastern states as Maine, Massachusetts, Pennsylvania, Rhode Island, and Vermont. Perhaps people are seeking warmer areas to the south.

By 1975 the South numbered 68 million, or about 32 percent of the population. The Northeast had 49 million. The North Central states, with 58 million, were less populous than the South, and the West was coming on strong with 38 million. So we can see from looking at these figures how business and industry would be vitally interested in the statistics. If one were in some area of real estate, for example, he would think of going west or south.

# HEALTH

According to the Statisical Abstract figures, Americans spent a total of $118.5 billion in 1975 on health care, about 8.2 percent of our Gross National Product. There were 121,000 medical schools, 58,000 dental schools, and 1,359 schools of nursing. Some 394,000 physicians and 124,000 dentists were practicing. Nurses totaled 857,000. This averaged out to about 153 doctors, 40 dentists, and 404 nurses for each 100,000 people.

Heart disease continued to be the leading killer in the United States, with 349.2 deaths per 100,000 of population in 1974. Cancer was second at 170.5; then cerebrovascular diseases at 98.1 followed by accidents, flu and pneumonia, diabetes, cirrhosis of the liver, arteriosclerosis, infant diseases, bronchitis, emphysema, and asthma.

There were 91,750 reported narcotics addicts in 1974, with an average age of 27.5 years. There were also 5,400,000 alcoholics in 1970, 4.5 million of them men, and 0.9 million women. Some 43,155,000 males over 17 smoked, compared to 18,626,000 who did not; 32,834,000 females smoked, and 41,202,000 did not. More than 2 million women and 4 million men reported smoking more than 35 cigarettes a day on a regular basis, in spite of the surgeon-general's warning.

# WELFARE

In 1975, total expenditures for social welfare (including social security, public aid, health and medical programs, veterans' programs, education, housing, and other) amounted to $286.5 billion. This was about 20 percent of the GNP, and more than 58 percent of total government outlay. Some 3 million households received Aid to Families with Dependent Children.

# CRIME

Most Americans could be classed as "good guys," but the inevitable bad apples were also numbered in censuses. Criminals cost us billions of dollars, thousands of lives, and untold suffering. Among its many surveys, the Bureau of the Census conducts the National

Crime Panel, a continuing sample survey of households and commercial establishments for the Law Enforcement Assistance Administration. It also gathers information from many other sources for its statistics on law enforcement.

In 1975 all levels of American government spent about $15 billion to finance the criminal justice system costing every man, woman, and child about $71. There were 539,409 state and local policemen, 3921 jails, and 592 state prisons, with 218,205 prisoners in these institutions. The total of reported crimes was 11,257,000, with 20,500 murders, 56,100 forcible rapes, 465,000 robberies, and 485,000 aggravated assaults. Although murders had nearly doubled since 1967, there had been no executions of murderers in the United States since then until 1977, when the state of Utah took the life of one killer.

More crime occurs in large cities than in suburban or rural areas. In towns under 10,000, there were 232 known offenses a year per 100,000 population. The percentage climbed steadily with increasing size until, for those of 250,000 or more, the figure was almost 5 times as high. Detroit led in crime, followed by Baltimore, Maryland; New York City; and Washington, D.C.

Murder statistics showed blacks and other minorities were victims 8 times as frequently as whites, considering their relative numbers. Males were murdered in 3 of 4 cases for whites, and 4 of 5 cases for blacks and others. Six times as many men as women were criminals. Suicides are considered crimes, and there were 25,683 in the United States in 1974, with about 3 times as many men killing themselves as women. Blacks and others committed about half as many suicides, considering relative numbers.

The most-used murder weapon was the gun. For every 120 shootings there were 30 stabbings, 10 killings with a blunt object, and 1 drowning. During 1975, civilians purchased a total of 6,852,000 guns of various types, with handguns being the most popular, followed by rifles and then shotguns. Officers made a total of 7,671,000 arrests in 1975, and 185 of them were killed in the line of duty.

# SUMMARY

Our census mirror reflects an interesting people whose material blessings have been increasing and who continue to move about within the nation. Radios are commonplace—the last census showed that each American family averages five of them. We spend more on cosmetics and tobacco than on private education and research; twice as much on recreation as on welfare and religion. And yet some segments of the population were mirrored as far from prosperous, the elderly, for example. Some 25 million Americans are over 65, with a median income of barely above $5,000. There were 35,000 marriages a year between Americans over 65; many of them do so to pool their meager incomes. Census records show that women live several years longer than men. But they also show that there are 3000 men over 65 who have married wives under 25 years of age, whereas only 2000 women over 55 have husbands that young.

California's Anaheim-Santa Ana-Garden Grove area, including Disneyland, increased in population by 551,000 from 1960 to 1970, while Pittsburgh, Pennsylvania, lost 167,000 of its residents. Three states—North Dakota, South Dakota, and West Virginia—also lost population. Though movement about the country continued, its mode changed. In 1970 there were more commercial airplane pilots than locomotive engineers. The railroads may have won the West, but it is the airlines that are making the money. With all our moving, however, 50 percent of us still lived within an hour's drive of an ocean or one of the Great Lakes.

The census, initiated to apportion the Congress, continues to do that, and the 1970 enumeration resulted in the redrawing of district boundaries in forty states. It also disclosed our political habits as not the most noble. In 1970, 13 percent of us falsely claimed to have voted in the previous election.

Yet with all our faults and all our grumbling about invasion of privacy and wasting our time, 85 percent of us returned our census questionnaires filled out and on time.

# 5
# Measure of the Nation

The chief instrument of American statistics is the census, which should accomplish a twofold object. It should serve the country, by making a full and accurate exhibit of the elements of national life and strength; and it should serve the science of statistics by so exhibiting general results that they may be compared with similar data obtained by other nations. The census is indispensable to modern statesmanship.

*President James A. Garfield*

We think first of counting *people* with a census, but many other kinds of information come from it as well. We learn how large our land is, how we are using it, and how well our government entities are faring. Paul Bunyan, that personification of American bigness, was a giant of a man who measured size by ax handles of heroic proportions. Paul must be proud of how the land of his adoption has grown. Beginning as a nation of immigrants clinging to the eastern seaboard, Americans have moved westward, multiplying in numbers and size. Like the legendary lumberjack, America is bursting its seams and has expanded beyond the continental boundaries.

The census measures the land that is our home, the farms and fields that make up our agricultural bounty (we feed much of the rest of the world), the dwellings that house all our millions of people, and the multitude of business and governmental entities so necessary to our economic and social business life. Military strength is also a measure of our nation, and the Bureau reports on that too.

# THE LAND

Americans share an admiration of size with most of the world's peoples. We want to be the biggest nation, with the largest cities, the tallest mountains, and the longest rivers. The United States first formally published information on state areas 130 years ago, and with the 1880 Census of Population, it established methods for accurate and detailed measurement of our country. Included were figures of the geographic extent of the United States and accurate maps of land and bodies of water.

*Areas of the United States: 1940* reported on land and water areas, counties, places, and minor civil divisions. This information was updated in the 1950 and 1960 censuses. In 1964, the Bureau added the measurement of places of at least 1,000 inhabitants, as well as county divisions used in the 1960 census.

With the addition of Alaska and Hawaii, the United States grew to a total of 3,628,066 square miles, all but 78,267 square miles of it dry land. Many of us believe that the federal govenment owns most of that land, but private land totals 1.3 billion acres, whereas "public land" (owned by federal, state and local governments) amounts to only 886 million acres. About 53 million acres are owned by Indians.

According to Census publications, 163 million acres are leased for grazing. Slightly more than 25 million acres have been set aside for parks and historic sites, and there are 226 million acres of National Forest lands.

Census reports reflect America's continuing love affair with camping and other outdoor pursuits. Most of us seem to savor our descent from rugged pioneers, and we like to return to such a life (or a pleasant approximation of it) as often as we can. Responding to this interest, in 1975 the federal government spent $270 million for additional outdoor recreational areas. The popularity of National Park facilities is indicated by the nearly 17 million overnight stays registered that year.

Although a visit to one of our more popular parks might suggest that a population explosion is a real danger, our land area is so large that if the 1970 population were evenly spread out over it, there would be only about fifty-eight of us on each square mile. China, hardly a highly urbanized society, has a density of about 200 inhabitants per square mile. There are an average of 720 Japanese in each square mile of that tiny nation, and the Netherlands is even more tightly packed with 812. The record-holder is Belgium, however, with 822 people per square mile.

The United States is well below the world's density of 68 per square mile. Alaska is our least settled state with only one person for each two square miles. Wyoming has 3.4 people per square mile, followed by Nevada with 4.4. and Montana with 4.8. The State of Washington, with a density of 51.2, comes closest to that of the country as a whole, and Alabama, at 67.9 has almost exactly the same density as the world's population as a whole. Since 1970, New Jersey has been our most crowded state at 953.1, considerably more than that of Belgium. However, Washington, D.C., is among the leaders for elbow-to-elbow Americans; population density in this congested district around the nation's capital is an amazing 12,402 people per square mile!

In 1790, only 1 in 20 was an urban dweller. In 1970, nearly three of every four Americans lived in and around large cities. A further difference in the population mix in our nation should be noted: suburban areas held 75.6 million people in 1970, for the first time more people than lived in the large central cities.

It is sometimes said that we became suburbanites because of the automobile and the mobility that wheels give us. The trend began between 1820 and 1840, however, and has continued at about the same pace ever since, with no sudden upsurge in 1908, when Henry Ford's Model T chugged into the picture. The car certainly didn't make it any harder to flee the central city or the farm, however. Today, it lets millions of us travel quickly from home to work and back again.

Census statistics tell us that six of seven suburbanites commute by private car. What is more surprising is that seven of ten people in the central cities do the same thing in spite of generally good urban transit systems. About 19 percent of big-city dwellers use the bus, streetcar, subway, or elevated train for transportation; only about 4 percent of suburbanites do.

# NATION ON THE MOVE

Transportation is one of America's strengths, and probably the single greatest influence on our way of life. Our 134 million motor vehicles have an excellent system of streets and highways to travel on; census figures show an unbelievable total of 3,730,082 miles of municipal and rural roads. America also has more that 13,000 public and private airports, serving almost 2,300 domestic and international airliners and a general aviation fleet of more than 161,000.

The old song asks, "How're you goin' to keep 'em down on the farm?" and the obvious answer is, you can't. We now have 153 cities of 100,000 or more people, up 23 from the 1960 census. Remarkably, 59 *lost* population as people drifted south and west. Houston joined the "super cities" with a population exceeding 1 million, giving America a total of six such "megalopoli." But Chicago, Philadelphia, and Detroit lost population between 1960 and 1970. To someone in an orbiting space craft, this clustering of population across our country is obvious at night in the light patterns of metropolitan areas. An interesting and accurate duplicate is produced in the Census Bureau's "night map" presentation of population areas.

# THE "CENTER OF POPULATION"

It is ironic that the *geographical center* of America is also the least settled area of the country, near the borders of Montana, Wyoming, and South Dakota. The point at which a flat cutout of the nation would balance is 17 miles due west of Castle Rock in Butte County, South Dakota.

Because population is not evenly distributed over the country, the *center of population* is some distance from the geographical center. This center is defined as "that point upon which the United States would balance if it were a rigid plane without weight and the population distributed thereon, with each individual being assumed to have equal weight and to exert an influence on a central point proportional to his distance from that point."

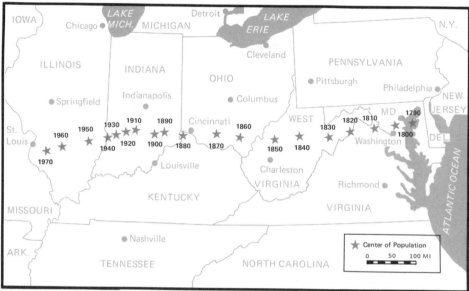

CENTER OF POPULATION FOR THE UNITED STATES: 1790 TO 1970

U.S. DEPARTMENT OF COMMERCE

BUREAU OF THE CENSUS

*Chart showing how the center of population has moved steadily west since 1790; by the mid-1980s, it may have leaped the Mississippi River.*

When the first census was taken in 1790, the center of population turned out to be near the town of Chestertown, Maryland, about 23 miles east of Baltimore. With each 10-year counting of westward-moving people, the center also moved west and slightly south. In 1800 it was west of Baltimore, and in 1810 had moved into Virginia. For the next four censuses, through 1850, the center marched across West Virginia and in 1860 was south and east of Columbus, Ohio. By 1880 it was near Cincinnati and close to the Indiana border, into which state it moved in 1890.

After slowing its pace from 1890 to 1940, the center of population picked up speed again as the American South and West began to grow much faster than the North and East. Between 1950 and 1960, the jump was an impressive 57 miles across Illinois.

Locating the 1970 population center was a complex geometrical process carried out by the U.S. Coast and Geodetic Survey. Using 250,000 geographical points representing areas of population in 1970, experts located the center in a soybean field about 5 miles southeast of Mascoutah, Illinois. To mark the site, Secretary of

100

Commerce Maurice Stans dedicated a stone standard with a suitably inscribed bronze plaque on the grounds of the Mascoutah City Hall.

The longest jump came in 1860, when the population center moved 80.6 miles. Shortest was in 1920, when it inched only 10 miles from the previous site. In 190 years the center has moved 701 miles west, but only 47 miles south; a safe guess is that is has now moved farther west and slightly south. The 1980 census will show us the exact spot upon which America would balance if there were 60 or so of us in each of its 3.6 million square miles.

## ENVIRONMENT

A true measure of the land reports not just geographical centers, area, and miles of rivers and highways, but also the environmental conditions existing in and over the land. The Bureau of the Census collects and presents such data to help us better understand the condition of our environment. Coordinating environmental quality programs in the United States is the Council on Environmental Quality. The Environmental Protection Agency conducts pollution research and enforces regulations against violators. The U.S. Public Health Service in 1957 established the National Air Surveillance Network with 94 urban and 30 rural locations. By 1974 there were more than 3,700 sampling stations in the United States.

The Bureau of the Census provides data on air and water pollution, and climate as well. Among the statistics appearing in census reports are the percentage of Americans drinking fluoridated water, national expenditures for pollution abatement and control, and sales of pesticides. Climatic information published for most cities includes information on freezing, average temperatures, rainfall and other precipitation statistics, percentage of sunshine, wind speeds, heating and cooling requirements, and humidity.

## GOVERNMENT STATISTICS

It is difficult to imagine life with no government. Many attempts at doing without have demonstrated that we need such a system to

101

guide us, and people in authority to lead us. This grows truer than ever as population climbs and life becomes more complex. Yet, if we can't live without government, it seems almost equally true that we have a difficult time living *with* it. Indeed, as we realize that we must work into the month of May before we have paid Uncle Sam and all the other tax collectors it is easy to imagine that the solution to the problem of living together may be worse than the problem itself.

Here again the Bureau of the Census performs a service in reporting on governments. Although such reports are largely for governments themselves, they are available to those who want to understand the system better. Although the Bureau is itself part of the federal government, it does not have a vested interest in what it reports. In fact, as a neutral observer, it provided the most objective information available on governments.

## The Federal Government

According to the Census Bureau's *Statistical Abstract*, in 1978 the United States Government had receipts of $402 billion and outlays totaling $451 billion. This deficit of a whopping $49 billion is a financial trick that only Uncle Sam can perform. The national debt was about $772 billion, more than double what it had been a decade earlier. Federal expenditures represented 25 percent of the Gross National Product. There were 2,875,000 civilian federal government employees, with a payroll of $50 billion.

Not surprisingly, we individual taxpayers contributed most of the dollars for financing government; individual income taxes amounted to 44 percent of the total. Next were social security taxes and contributions, at 31 percent. Corporate income taxes came to 14 percent of the total; excise and other taxes made up the remaining 9 percent.

## State and Local Governments

Nationwide statistics on state and local governments, including employees, finances, and other data, are compiled regularly by the Bureau of the Census. Every five years, in years ending in 2 and 7, the Bureau conducts the Census of Governments. It also makes annual surveys covering all state governments, plus a sample of local governments. Publications resulting from these many surveys are described in a pamphlet titled *Recurrent Publications on Governments*.

We think of the federal government as "big government," but it is even more mind-boggling to learn the magnitude of state and local governments. The 1977 Census of Governments listed 79,913 local governments: counties, municipalities, townships, school districts, and a host of "special" districts including such entities as housing authorities, port authorities, power districts, and irrigation districts. The 1978 revenue of all governments was $732 billion. Of this, $430 billion was federal, $172 billion state, and $130 billion local. In 1978 there were 12,743,000 state and local government employees in the United States. Their total payroll for just the month of October that year was $12,139,000,000.

The first census data collected on "government statistics," gathered for the 1840 census, involved numbers and kinds of schools and students. Later censuses included property values, local taxes, schools, utility systems, the public debt, and public finance. More recently have come data on governmental income and expenditures, and estimates of national wealth by state and class of property.

The Census of Population in 1850 included statistics on state and local governments. In 1902 (the year the Bureau of the Census was established) a separate Census of Governments was taken. In 1957, the first 5-year Census of Governments was taken. These list all governments and gather facts including finances and employment. Detailed figures are obtained from larger local governments and from the 50 states, permitting the Bureau of the Census to publish accurate statistics on government organization, public employment, and government financial affairs.

## GEOGRAPHICAL AREAS

Census data are reported for areas of government of greatly varying size. The largest is the United States itself, of course. This includes the fifty states and the District of Columbia, plus outlying areas under United States sovereignty and jurisdiction. Next come the four census regions: West, South, Northeast, and North Central. Each of these regions includes two or more geographic divisions, or groupings of states. There are nine such divisions.

The nation's governmental units are covered by the Bureau in its censuses, surveys, and special reports. Besides the fifty states, these include congressional districts, counties, and Minor Civil Divisions, or MCDs, which include towns and townships, incorporated places, and wards. In the twenty-one states where MCDs are not adequate for accurately reporting census statistics, the Census Bureau and local officials have established Census County Divisions, or CCDs.

Next is the Standard Metropolitan Statistical Area, or SMSA, beloved of city planners. An SMSA is a central city or twin cities of at least 50,000 inhabitants plus adjacent counties integrated economically and socially with the central city or cities. In New England, cities take the place of counties. In 1976, 73.2 percent of us lived within SMSAs. The Urban Atlas Series present 1970 census data by census tract for the 65 SMSAs with more than 500,000 population.

Urban Areas, or UAs, are made up of a central city or cities, plus the surrounding suburbs.

Unincorporated places are concentrations of population not incorporated into cities or villages. The Bureau of the Census works with local authorities in defining such unincorporated places.

Census Tracts, or CTs, are convenient statistical subdivisions of counties. These tracts have as close to 4,000 inhabitants as is practicable.

Enumeration Districts, or EDs, are those areas within a tract, MCD, or other area that will be canvassed by one census enumerator. In the 1970 census, enumeration districts averaged about 750 inhabitants.

Block Groups, or BGs, are city blocks in large urban areas grouped into units of about 1,000 inhabitants each.

Blocks are generally just that—city or town blocks bounded by streets or other physical features. They are where we live.

Two specialized areas used by the Bureau of the Census in its retail trade surveys and censuses are Central Business Districts, or CBDs, and Major Retail Centers, or MRCs.

So many maps, and what importance do they have, anyway? A

map actually seems like a cold and impersonal arrangement of lines having little to do with the human equation of the census. In reality, however, it can be very personal, even vital to those whose business it is to interpret maps and the numbers that go with them. An easy way to show this is with colored pencils.

In the book, *This U.S.A.*, Richard Scammon, then director of the Census Bureau, described how he personalized the squares and other shapes of census maps simply by shading them with colored pencils.

"That's Saginaw, Michigan," he told the book's narrator, "but it's not only Saginaw, it's almost every city in America. I've never yet shaded a city where income—the red—and education—the yellow—don't overlap to a great degree, and I've never seen an American city where either the red or the yellow area touches much of the blue—the Negro area."

Scammon could also deftly show that most "good," high-income, neighborhoods in America's large cities lie on the west or north side of town. He had no answer for this phenomenon, but someday a researcher will solve the puzzle and perhaps also learn something of value to the human inhabitants of all those SMSAs, MCDs, and BGs.

The Bureau of the Census produces a variety of maps covering all these areas. Included are all the 3,141 counties or equivalents existing at the time of the 1970 census, metropolitan area maps of SMSAs, tract-outline maps, urbanized area maps, county subdivision maps, place maps for every incorporated and unincorporated place not included in the Metropolitan Map Series, and Central Business District/Major Retail Center maps.

The Bureau also produces GBF/DIME (Geographic Base File/ Dual Independent Map Encoding) files used for a number of purposes including city planning, schools, and business. Much data is also available as computer programs and tapes. Included are ADMATCH and UNIMATCH; MEDlist (the Master Enumeration District); DIMECO, a boundary file of counties in the 48 coterminous states; Centers of Population; PICADAD, a computer list of place names and associated geographic codes and coordinates; and other programs.

# ELECTIONS

The original purpose of the U.S. census was to apportion our congressional representatives. The census continues to serve this function. Since 1912 the number of representatives has remained fixed at 435, except for the 1960–1962 period, when the addition of Alaska and Hawaii as states temporarily increased the total to 437.

In 1970, Arizona's growing population had earned it another Congressman. For months, state legislators pored over maps and punched buttons on computers as they carved out a new district that favored the controlling majority. The 1980 census will authorize another such division to make four districts into five.

In addition to Congressional representation, the census also reflects the American citizen's interest in the voting right our Founding Fathers left us. Unfortunately, our record is not good. As an election aid, the Bureau of the Census provides estimates of the voting population in each state, by age group and race, for presidential and congressional election years. Estimates are also made of the percent of the population casting votes. Census records of voting in presidential elections and in off-election years tell an interesting story. Presidential elections historically pull 10 to 12 percent more voters to polls than do other elections. In 1960, for example, when John F. Kennedy was elected President, 58.5 percent of Americans of voting age turned out. Two years later, only 45.4 percent voted for congressional representatives.

There is evidence that voters may be disenchanted with the election process as a result of Watergate and other scandals. In 1968, 77 percent of those of voting age were registered. For the 1972 presidential election this dropped to 72.3 percent, and in 1976 only 66.7 percent registered to vote. More detailed breakdowns by voter characteristics show that 18-to-20-year-olds recently given the right to vote have the poorest voting record. In 1972, more than half did not vote. The 1974 turnout was worse, with nearly 80 percent not voting. Only one young person in five participated in the important process of electing government officials and voting on other issues.

Other interesting information can be found in Bureau election statistics. In 1974, for instance, only 34 percent of those with less than 8 years of schooling voted, whereas 55 percent of those with more than 12 years of schooling voted. Southerners turned in a poor voting record in 1974, with 36 percent going to the polls, compared with 49 percent for the North and West. Only 29 percent of the unemployed voted, while 47 percent of those with jobs turned out.

Happily, there are brighter spots in voting statistics. The impact of civil-rights legislation and enforcement on voting populations in the South has been measured by Bureau statistics from 1960 to 1975. In 1960, only 29 percent of blacks were registered to vote in eleven southern states. By 1975 more than 58 percent of the black population registered, almost equal to the percentage of white registered voters. The Bureau continues to check on voter registration.

## HOUSING

According to the old saying, our homes are our castles. But housing is more than a roof over our heads; it is big business too, and means jobs for many Americans. Housing is important to city planners and to school superintendents trying to prepare for the student population some years down the road. As we well know, housing is also important to the tax collector. For all these reasons, the Census Bureau is vitally concerned with accurately measuring housing in America.

There was no curiosity on the part of census takers concerning housing in the 1790 census. Indeed, it was 1860 before a single question was asked on that subject, and then it was asked about the number of slave houses. Two censuses later, enumerators asked about housing on Indian reservations, and in 1890 some general questions on housing were added to the census form.

During the next four censuses, through 1920, Americans were asked if they lived on farms, whether housing they owned was occupied or vacant, and if the houses they owned were mortgaged. In 1940 the first separate census of housing was taken, with many more questions asked. Users of census housing data include federal, state, and local government planners and administrators. In

107

the business sector, bankers, insurers, contractors, forest and mineral industries, manufacturers, wholesalers' and retailers' marketing organizations, chambers of commerce, and utility companies also use census housing statistics to improve their profits.

After World War II, the Bureau began supplementing Housing Census data with special surveys. These have included housing vacancy, residential finance, inventory change, market absorption of apartments, and annual housing surveys. The first annual housing survey was conducted in 1973, with reports published in 1975.

Using available historical records, the Bureau can trace the development of the construction industry since 1868. However, the Bureau did not begin collecting and publishing actual statistics on construction until 1930. These were part of the Business Census through 1939, then there was a lapse of nearly three decades before such statistics were resumed. In 1967, the Census of Construction became part of the Economic Censuses, which are taken every five years. Annual, monthly, and quarterly surveys are taken of construction, demolition, repairs and alterations, and values of certain types of construction.

Private housing starts in 1977 totaled about 2 million, continuing the rising trend since the deep construction slump of 1974–1975. This is still lower than the record high of 2.4 million private housing starts in 1973. Only "housing units," defined by the Bureau as a group of rooms or a single room intended for occupancy as separate living quarters are reported in the Housing Census. Transient accommodations, barracks for workers or the military, institutional quarters and vacant "mobile homes" are not counted.

All respondents are asked:

Number of units at this address
Complete kitchen and bathroom facilities
Whether owned or rented
Value or rental charge
Vacancy status and number of months vacant

From 1960 to 1970, the population increased by a sizable 13 percent, but housing units increased 18 percent. Here is an exam-

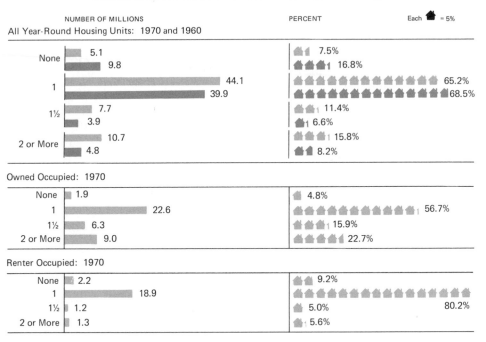

COMPLETE BATHROOMS FOR EXCLUSIVE USE: ■ 1970 AND ■ 1960

NUMBER OF MILLIONS
All Year-Round Housing Units: 1970 and 1960

PERCENT

Each 🏠 = 5%

| | | |
|---|---|---|
| None | 5.1 | 7.5% |
| | 9.8 | 16.8% |
| 1 | 44.1 | 65.2% |
| | 39.9 | 68.5% |
| 1½ | 7.7 | 11.4% |
| | 3.9 | 6.6% |
| 2 or More | 10.7 | 15.8% |
| | 4.8 | 8.2% |

Owned Occupied: 1970

| | | |
|---|---|---|
| None | 1.9 | 4.8% |
| 1 | 22.6 | 56.7% |
| 1½ | 6.3 | 15.9% |
| 2 or More | 9.0 | 22.7% |

Renter Occupied: 1970

| | | |
|---|---|---|
| None | 2.2 | 9.2% |
| 1 | 18.9 | 80.2% |
| 1½ | 1.2 | 5.0% |
| 2 or More | 1.3 | 5.6% |

*Bathrooms are the subject of this chart, based on the 1960 and 1970 censuses, showing that 62.5 percent of us command at least one private bath and 15.8 percent have two or more.*

ple of census data telling us important things. More new houses than new people means that fewer of us are living in each house, and that some houses are lived in for only part of the year. Perhaps 1 million new houses were second homes built by people with the money for such luxuries.

"Mobile homes" are growing in popularity. They are generally cheaper to buy and can be moved. In 1970 there were almost 250,000 of them in the Northeast, about 500,000 in the North Central region and in the West, and nearly 900,000 in the South. Although no census can be perfectly accurate, estimates are that the margin of error in housing counts for 1970 was only 1.7 percent.

109

# AGRICULTURE

Although America began as a nation made up largely of farmers, three censuses went by before even the sketchiest information was collected about this majority of the population. In 1820, the population census noted the people engaged in farming, but not until 1840 was a meaningful Census of Agriculture taken. This lag stemmed from a reluctance on the part of farmers—and their elected representatives—to answer "prying" questions on the census form. The questions on the first Census of Agriculture were very limited: number of farm animals, how much wool was produced, kinds and quantities of crops, and value of farm products and poultry.

Of the many changes that have taken place in America in the last 150 years, perhaps none is more important than the change in the relative size of the farm population. In 1820, census takers listed a total of slightly more than 2.5 million people in the American labor force. Of these, 349,000 were in the manufacturing trades; another 72,000 were employed in commerce. All the rest, well over 2 million Americans, were farmers. Nearly 85 percent of Americans in 1820 still worked on farms; only about 1 in 7 had another kind of job. By 1970, however, the employment picture had been turned upside down. Although the total population had grown dramatically from 4 million to 203 million, the number of farm workers was little more than it had been in 1790.

Even though only a handful of us are involved in farming, information about agriculture is of increasing importance. Censuses of Agriculture were taken along with Censuses of Population until 1920, when it was decided that an accounting of what was happening on the nation's farms was needed twice as often. Censuses of Agriculture were taken in years ending in "4" and "9" until a 1976 law provided for them in 1978 and 1982, and then every five years after that.

The first censuses of farming were conducted in person by having a census taker visit each farm, ask questions, and make out a report form. After 1950, however, questionnaires were mailed to farmers and an enumerator called later to collect and check the completed forms. With the 1969 census, mail was used both ways, with personal follow-ups only if needed. In 1974 even this personal

110

touch was eliminated as follow-ups began to be done by telephone or mail.

In addition to the 5-year agriculture censuses, the Bureau conducts special agriculture surveys, principally the Cotton Survey, which dates back to 1902 and has been taken every year since. As a result, we have accurate information on farming for the nation as a whole, by region, state and county.

To qualify as a farm, a plot of ground must consist of more than 10 acres, with sales of at least $50 annually, or under 10 acres with sales at least $250 annually. All such plots are recorded in the census every five years. Included as farms are nurseries, greenhouses, hothouses, sod farms, mushroom houses, and cranberry bogs. Not included are forests, fisheries, and poultry not grown in captivity.

In 1935 there were the most farms ever counted—6,812,350; there were only 2,314,013 farms in 1974. The total value of all farms in 1974 was about $342 billion, with an average value per farm of $147,838. Crop values per year ranged from only $7 per acre in Nye County, Nevada, to $1,231 per acre in Suffolk County, New York.

The total acreage of all farms in the United States was slightly more than 1 billion, with an average of 387 acres, more than double the average in 1930. The amount of land in agriculture has decreased by more than a hundred million acres in 20 years, as average farm size increases and the small farmer fades away.

Total farm-product gross receipts in 1975 amounted to $101.5 billion, and the United States exported about $21.3 billion in agricultural products, against imports of about $9.5 billion. The principal crops include cotton, hay, and lettuce in Arizona; corn, peanuts, soybeans, and tobacco in Georgia; potatoes, hay, and apples in Rhode Island; and hay, sugar beets, wheat, and barley in Wyoming.

Don't go into farming because you think there's no paperwork. When the Census of Agriculture began, farmers were asked the number of cattle, milch cows, and oxen; they were also asked about the production of cheese, gallons of wine, pounds of silk cocoons, and bushels of Indian corn. In 1974, dozens of questions were asked about acreage and value, land use, crop acreage and production,

111

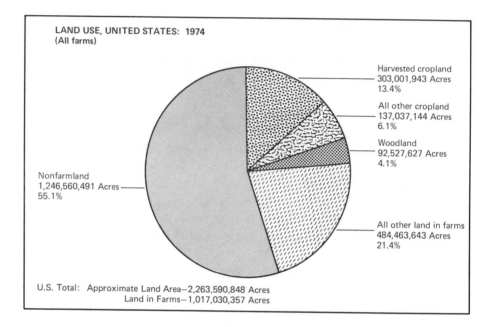

LAND USE, UNITED STATES: 1974
(All farms)

Harvested cropland
303,001,943 Acres
13.4%

All other cropland
137,037,144 Acres
6.1%

Woodland
92,527,627 Acres
4.1%

Nonfarmland
1,246,560,491 Acres
55.1%

All other land in farms
484,463,643 Acres
21.4%

U.S. Total:  Approximate Land Area—2,263,590,848 Acres
Land in Farms—1,017,030,357 Acres

*A pie chart from the 1970s shows that nearly half of all our land is occupied by farms or woodlands.*

irrigation and drainage, fertilizer and pesticide use, livestock and poultry production, machinery and equipment, contracts and marketing agreements, payroll and employment, injuries and illnesses, farm debts, value of products sold, production expenses, fuel and grain storage, cotton ginning, baling, combining, crop dusting, plowing, veterinary services, commercial hunting and trapping, age, race, residence, and more!

Who needs all this farm information? Many people and organizations do. The Department of Agriculture uses it for year-to-year estimates and projections. Federal, state, and local agencies use the information in planning rural development, research, and extension work. Congress uses it for revising existing farm programs and devising new ones. Farm cooperatives, trade associations, and "agribusinesses" use census agricultural data in forecasting markets, locating new plants and service centers, and in advertising

112

and other marketing decisions. Although the Bureau admits that most individual farmers probably never see a census publication, it also feels they all benefit from the statistics it produces.

## THE MILITARY

For national defense in 1976, the United States spent about $93 billion; veterans' benefits amounted to $19 billion. The entire world exported about $8.4 billion in arms; the United States accounted for $3.8 billion of this, or about 45 percent of the total.

Wars the United States has participated in have cost:

| | |
|---|---|
| World War II | $530 billion |
| Vietnam | 118 billion |
| Korea | 68 billion |
| World War I | 49 billion |
| Civil War | |
| (Union costs only) | 6.5 billion |
| Spanish-American | 2.5 billion |
| American Revolution | 148 million |
| War of 1812 | 127 million |
| Mexican | 109 million |
| Total | $774.4 billion |

In 1975 there were about 2,180,000 men and women in the armed forces with an additional 1,039,000 in defense-related agencies, for a total of 3,219,000. The military payroll was $35 billion. There were 97,000 women in the armed forces, 14,000 of them officers. There were 302,000 blacks, 9,000 of them officers. Here is a "population census" of our military:

*Military Personnel*

| | |
|---|---|
| Army | 782,000 |
| Navy | 525,000 |
| Marines | 196,000 |
| Air Force | 584,000 |

113

# CENSUS

The census obviously is far more than the commonly thought of "people count." It is truly a measure of the land as well, a measure that includes geographical bounds, environment, agriculture, government entities, and other institutions. That this monumental task is done well is a tribute to the Census Bureau and its wide-ranging men and women.

# 6
# Gauge of the Economy

Billions of our dollars now ride on the accuracy of our monthly unemployment report.

*Maurice Stans*
*Budget Director under President Eisenhower*

Demographers at the Bureau of the Census are sure that people
are the key. Without people, they ask, what else can make any
difference? For them, the censuses of population and housing are of
prime importance. Census people in Economic Fields, however,
make a strong case for their censuses as vital contributors to our
welfare and even our survival in an increasingly complex world.

The dictionary defines economics as "a social science concerned
chiefly with description and analysis of the production, distribution, and consumption of goods and services." Money is not mentioned, but it is a fact of economic life that money is the quickest
gauge of how well or poorly the process is succeeding. To us as
individuals, the ratio of our money's outgo to income is of vital
importance, not only in the marketplace but particularly in our
private lives. Money may not be everything but it surely helps, so it
is not surprising that the Bureau of the Census compiles and publishes a wealth of information about the dollar and related matters.

115

# THE ALMIGHTY DOLLAR

One starting point in discussing economics is that magic number called the Gross National Product, or GNP. This is defined as the total national output of goods and services at market prices. The question is sometimes raised as to how accurate the GNP is, since there might be transactions like the classic swap of a $50,000 dog for two $25,000 cats! Nevertheless, the GNP is a useful benchmark in gauging the state of the economy.

For years a $1 trillion (a thousand billion) GNP was eagerly anticipated by those to whom such mileposts are important. A trillion one-dollar bills, by the way, would make a stack 80 miles high. That first trillion-dollar GNP came in 1971, when the total went about 63 billion above the goal. And by 1975 it had been exceeded by 50 percent with a GNP of about $1.5 trillion. The largest category in the 1975 GNP was our "disposable personal income," amounting to slightly more than $1 trillion. Next was government (federal, state, and local) at $274 billion; business, with $183 billion; and foreign business amounting to about $29 billion.

*The Almighty Dollar*

Two factors drive the GNP upward every year. The population and the business it generates are both growing. There is also inflation, which at the beginning of 1980 was raising costs over 10 percent a year. A "price deflator" adjustment applied to the GNP in 1975 dropped it from $1.5 trillion to just under $1.2 trillion. This adjustment was to "constant dollars" rather than current dollars. There have been a few years in which the constant dollar GNP actually dropped from the previous year, such as in 1974 and 1975, when decreases of 1.7 and 1.8 percent occurred, respectively.

The Gross National Product dollar figure has little meaning to us as individuals but it can be cut down to size: In 1975, every American was worth $7,016 as his share of the GNP. In its "Statistical Abstract," the Bureau of the Census even tells how each of us spent our share of the GNP. Statistics for 1950 and 1974 also give an indication of how life-styles and costs have changed during the last quarter century.

| Category | 1950 | 1974 |
|---|---|---|
| Food, beverages, tobacco | 30.3% | 22.9% |
| Clothes, accessories, jewelry | 12.3% | 8.6% |
| Personal care | 1.3% | 1.5% |
| Housing | 11.3% | 15.4% |
| Household operation | 15.2% | 14.7% |
| Medical care | 4.7% | 8.6% |
| Personal business | 3.4% | 5.0% |
| Transportation | 13.2% | 13.0% |
| Recreation | 5.8% | 6.8% |
| Other | 2.5% | 3.5% |

Today we spend about 7 percent less on food, beverages, and tobacco, yet our medical bills have increased by 4 percent. We have also cut clothes, accessories, and jewelry about 4 percent while hiking the amounts for housing by about an equal amount. Such adjustments tell us many things about ourselves and our society. For example, either we are eating less (not likely), or food prices have held better than we all thought. We might think, to look at medical costs, that we were all sicker, but examining it more closely, we find that doctor and hospital costs have risen faster than overall inflation.

In 1976, Americans were paying off mortgages totaling $741 billion, and the total public debt was nudging $3 trillion, double the GNP! Consumer credit was about $197 billion. Not all business was done on credit, of course, and United States money in circulation totaled about $87 billion, with $55 billion in coins and small bills, and $32 billion in large denominations. Although there were 400 $10,000 bills in circulation, it is doubtful that many Americans had ever seen one of these expensive portraits of Salmon P. Chase.

In 1960 the U.S. Mint produced about 2.8 billion coins of various values. By 1975 coin production was up to about 13.5 billion, including 5 million bicentennial silver dollars and 10 *billion* pennies! The minting of 10 billion pennies does not square with rumors that that modest coin is to be dropped from our money system.

We Americans have billions of dollars to invest and have put lots of it to work in business. Stocks and bonds were sold in the amount of $167 billion on registered exchanges in 1975. Stock ownership is interesting:

| | |
|---|---|
| Male | 12,698,000 |
| Female | 12,508,000 |
| Under 21 | 1,818,000 |
| 21–34 | 2,838,000 |
| 35–44 | 3,976,000 |
| 45–54 | 5,675,000 |
| 55–64 | 5,099,000 |
| 65 plus | 5,800,000 |
| Total Investors | 25,206,000 |

## PRICES

Most of us realize that as wages rise, so do prices, since wages are such a large factor in the cost of goods. In 1890, the Bureau of Labor Statistics first established the "Wholesale Price Index," which measures average changes in prices of all commodities. There is also a "Consumer Price Index," with a section on food prices. It is these sources the Census Bureau uses.

The Bureau has computed the purchasing power of the United States dollar from 1940 to the present, using 1967 as the base period. Today, we pay about 2.5 times as much for goods as we did in 1940. Rents also increase as the years go by. The $75-a-month apartment of 1950 census reports now costs $200. Utilities and fuels have more than doubled in the quarter century just passed. And we don't need census figures to realize that energy costs will probably increase much faster than general inflation.

The dollar, of course, is only the highly visible tip of the iceberg. To see beneath the dollar sign we must look at the goods and services that make up manufacturing, mineral industries, agriculture, domestic trade, foreign trade, construction, and transportation.

## CENSUS OF MANUFACTURES AND INDUSTRY

The American Colonial censuses, taken before we became a nation, were conducted by the British Board of Trade. That body realized the importance of accurate knowledge of industry and sales. Several legislators involved in planning the first American census in 1790 argued strongly for the gathering of such information. They knew it would benefit our new nation, which might soon be in direct competition with England for trade. Part of the reason our Founding Fathers failed to give permission for gathering these statistics was the fact that America was born an agricultural nation. But even in the area of farming, early censuses barely scratched the surface and were of limited value to the government or anyone else.

By 1810, however, the American Congress was aware of an industrial economy that hinted it might rival farming. As a result, an act was passed directing the federal marshals and their census-taking assistants to "take an account of the several manufacturing establishments and manufacturers within their several divisions." This pioneer program gathered information in 27 broad categories of manufacturing, and cataloged more than 200 kinds of goods. It was extended in 1840 to include mineral industries as well (the California Gold Rush was only a few years away).

As James Madison and others who had urged such enumerations expected, America by the turn of the twentieth century had become the greatest industrial nation in the world. No longer a ragtag band of farmers fighting off redcoats with pitchforks, they had matured as manufacturers and industrialists. The censuses had helped bring business success, and success in turn guaranteed the expansion of the enumeration effort. A first step was to halve the time between manufacturing censuses, taking them every five years. This pace continued until 1919, when the censuses were taken every other year (until the pressures of World War II required a continuous series of war-related surveys).

Five-year censuses are now taken of manufactures and of mineral industries. In addition, continuing surveys include reports on major industrial categories. The Census of Manufactures covers about 450 industries ranging from bakeries to blast furnaces. Five mining-industry groups (metal mining, anthracite mining, bituminous coal and lignite mining, oil and gas extraction, and the mining and quarrying of nonmetallic minerals except fuels) are broken further into 42 industries for the Census of Mineral Industries. Close to $19 billion of income came from the mineral industries in 1975.

The Annual Survey of Manufactures samples about 70,000 of the approximate total of 320,000 manufacturing businesses in the United States employing about 20 million of us Americans. For example, in a recent year the beverage industry employed about 212,000 people and produced $14 billion in products. The tobacco industry manufactured 627 billion cigarettes, or about 3,000 apiece for every man, woman, and child in the United States, in spite of the U.S. Surgeon General's often repeated warning that cigarettes are harmful to health! For good measure, there were 8.3 billion cigars and 151 million pounds of tobacco produced.

The garment industry manufactured nearly 2 billion pounds of knit cloth in 1975, and turned that into 13.3 million dozen sweaters and jackets, 47.3 million dozen sport shirts, 134 million dozen dresses, 7.6 million dozen skirts, and 20 million coats. A total of 97.7 million dozen pairs of women's hose were also produced.

## THE BUSINESS CENSUSES

In spite of the great importance attached to manufacturing and industry, Congress lagged in providing similar reporting of business statistics. Although a small amount of business information was collected in the 1840 census, it was 1930 before the initiation of the first censuses of retail and wholesale trade. A census of "selected service industries" was added in 1933. This gathered information from garages, hotels, places of amusements, dental laboratories, and other service establishments. The Great Depression of the 1930's led to broader and more comprehensive censuses of business in 1935 and 1939. These provided the first factual appraisal of the effects of a serious business depression.

As with censuses of manufacturing and industry, business censuses were replaced during World War II by ongoing surveys related to wartime needs. The future seemed bright for business censuses, after their very late start, but a shock was in store for the Bureau: in 1953, the Secretary of Commerce came close to abolishing business censuses for lack of governmental interest and fear of "overburdening businesses with forms to fill out." It was the businessmen themselves who saved the day by urging not just the continuance of the censuses but their expansion. A subsequent attempt to curtail business censuses by the Office of Management and Budget was also defeated in the early 1970's. This required hearings before Congress, with both businessmen and Census officials testifying on the importance of such censuses and the need for their continuance.

In 1954 the quinquennial or 5-year economic census program was inaugurated, including the censuses of manufacturing, mineral industries, retail trade, wholesale trade, and selected service industries. Censuses of transportation and construction have since been added, with the entire series taken in years ending in 2 and 7. In addition to the economic censuses, the Bureau conducts monthly and annual Retail Trade Surveys, Wholesale Trade Surveys, a Selected Service Industry Survey, an Annual Survey of Manufactures, Current Industrial Reports, and others.

The business censuses include Retail Trade: places of business selling merchandise for personal or household consumption;

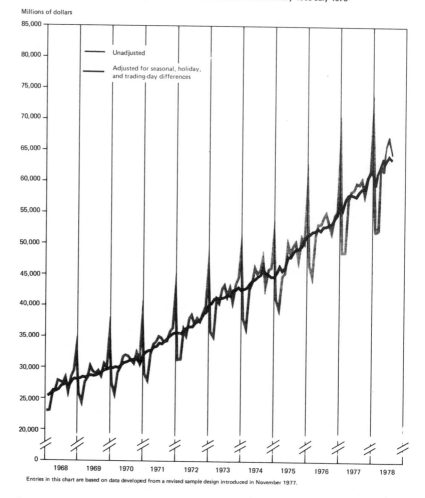

Estimated Monthly Retail Sales for the United States: January 1968-July 1978

Millions of dollars

——— Unadjusted

——— Adjusted for seasonal, holiday, and trading-day differences

1968  1969  1970  1971  1972  1973  1974  1975  1976  1977  1978

Entries in this chart are based on data developed from a revised sample design introduced in November 1977.

*The rise and fall of retail sales over the decade 1968-1978. Recording such records enables the Census Bureau to keep merchants informed and able to make long-term business plans.*

Wholesale Trade: establishments selling goods to dealers and distributors for resale or to purchasers who buy for business and farm use; and Selected Service Industries: engaged primarily in the sale of services as contrasted with the sale of merchandise.

In 1977 American consumers spent approximately $723 billion, in wholesale and retail trade. Most of the money went to food stores, followed closely by automobile dealers and general-merchandise stores. Restaurants and gasoline were next, then building materials, furnishings, clothing stores, drugstores, and liquor stores. Does that agree with the priorities in your budget?

The Census of Selected Service Industries covers more than 150 kinds of business and personal services. Service establishments totaled about 1,835,000. Service industries include lodging, laundry, beauty and barber shops, auto and other repair shops, motion pictures, amusements, recreation, and advertising. The receipts of service industries in 1977 totaled almost $180 billion.

Business statistics give key information about the American economy, including the current situation and projections for the future. All levels of government require such information, and business is using it increasingly. For example, trade organizations, market researchers, chambers of commerce, manufacturers, importers, distributors, retailers, and wholesalers are users, as will be described in a later chapter.

As with the population and housing censuses, response to the economic censuses is mandatory (except for short-term surveys), and inevitably there are some complaints from businessmen. These include questionnaires too large for typewriters, questions that are too nosy, and questions requiring time that could be better used working on business itself. Keenly sensitive to this "response burden," the Bureau works continually to reduce it. For example, only sample surveys are taken of one-owner small businesses, most of whom are not required to complete forms. Effort is also made to be sure that all the information taken is useful—often to the businessman himself. As a result, census forms are generally a blessing rather than a chore. Indeed, some companies use the forms for their own internal record-keeping.

## FOREIGN TRADE

We Americans buy many things from foreign countries; we also sell many things in the foreign market. For example, we buy about half of our petroleum from other countries, and we sell such things as computers and aircraft. The trick is to sell more than we buy, thus keeping a favorable "balance of trade." Mostly because of our oil imports, we have had unfavorable trade balances in recent years.

Foreign trade statistics are vital to the federal government for its balance-of-payments accounts, and for many other programs. Private industry, finance, research, transportation, and other fields also require this information. Applications include market analysis and market penetration studies, product and market development, measurement of competition, and future planning.

Foreign trade statistics were compiled for the first census back in 1790 and monthly data have been compiled since 1866. Until 1941 the Department of the Treasury had the responsibility of compiling these statistics; since that time the Bureau of the Census has prepared them. The Trade Act of 1974 requires that United States export information be directly related to our imports, and that both be related to domestic output. This has also been made compatible with the Standard International Trade Classification developed by the United Nations and used by most of the world-trading community.

## SUMMARY

Few of us who respond to the population and housing questions we receive every ten years have full understanding of the reasons for all those questions and how they are put to use in improving life for us. Many more of those responding to the Bureau's economic censuses do have such an understanding. Like the gasoline tax that pays for highways and streets (and is thus easy to understand and more palatable), the economic censuses make sense to most businessmen who must participate in them. Even for those of us not engaged in business, it is clear that if we are to have a stable economy, with jobs and people pretty well matched up most of the time, we must have an accurate report of what and how business is doing. Once again, it is the census that makes such reporting possible.

# 7
# Population Tomorrow

There is no government in history that has ever had any effect on population. One of the nice things about people is that they don't pay too much
attention to government, particularly with respect to the number of children they have.

Daniel P. Moynihan

The "population clock" in the Commerce Building in Washington, D.C., ticks away an ever-increasing population instead of the
passage of minutes. Set to tick at the current rate of increase, it is an
impressive demonstration of our rapidly increasing population. At
the date of the 1980 census, America had a population of
222,566,632.

Statistics presently governing our population change are:

1 birth each 8 seconds
1 death each 17 seconds
1 immigration each 60 seconds
1 emigration every 15 seconds

Adding and subtracting these inputs gives a net population gain of 1
American each 15 seconds, or about 2 million a year. It would seem
that all the Bureau has to do is multiply by the number of seconds,
or years at that rate and make an accurate projection. But fertility,

125

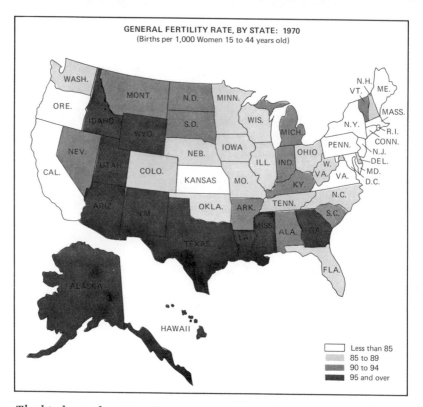

Less than 85
85 to 89
90 to 94
95 and over

*The birth rate by states, figures derived from the 1970 census. Compare this with the chart on page 92, showing population shifts.*

mortality, and arrivals and departures are constantly changing for a variety of unpredictable reasons. Wars cut population growth, periods after wars increase it again. And the increasing tendency of women to enter the career field obviously lowers the birth rate.

In 1935, in the middle of the Great Depression, the birth rate in the United States was at the very low figure of 18.7 per 1000. When the Depression ended, World War II was in progress, and this also tended to hold down growth. By 1945, a decade after its low in the Depression, the birth rate had increased only to 20.5. But in 1946 it jumped as war veterans returned home. By 1955 the birth rate had reached 24.9, and authorities began to be concerned about a population explosion that would swamp our schools and eventually flood our nation with more people than we could handle. What they did not take into account was that birth rates fluctuate widely. In 1800, for example, the birth rate was more than double the alarming 24.9 of 1955, but by 1910 it had declined by more than half.

# THE QUEST FOR ZPG

A population census is not merely a catalog of past performance, it is also a method of planning for the future. The widely publicized "baby boom" after World War II undoubtedly had an effect on married couples in the years following. As a result, the birth rate has gradually decreased until in 1978 it was only 15.3, much lower than during the Depression. With the current death rate and other factors, this results in only 1.8 children for the average female during her lifetime, not enough to maintain a stable population. Before you exult or worry, however, there is sufficient "lag" in the population-producing system that a leveling-off would not show up until well into the twenty-first century. Although population increase has been slowed, we are still decades away from the zero population growth, or ZPG, advocated by some.

As has often been pointed out, population is not a mechanically controlled number that inexorably grows or declines. Instead, population is the result of *human* activity. And humans change their rate of increase in response to a variety of social, economic, and other factors.

Of great interest to those concerned with population is the fact that young married women are putting off having children for several years. While the effect this delay will have on the population remains to be seen, childless women are more likely to enter, or remain in, the world of work.

The birth rate is not the only controlling statistic for population. Nobody lives forever; deaths tend to balance births. The Bible says Methuselah lived 969 years, but there came a time in history when the average life span was 30 years, or even less. We have mentioned a very high birth rate in 1800. Balancing that birth rate was a death rate that today would be considered catastrophic. Since 1800, however, we have learned how to stay alive longer—the current average expectancy is about 73 years—and the death rate per 1000 population is about 9.5. Life expectancy has increased as the birth rate has gone down.

Two events could drastically affect population in the short term. One would be the occurrence of a wide-scale catastrophe such as nuclear war that kills millions of people, or a plague that has the same effect. A nuclear holocaust might also include genetic effects that would reduce births for a long time in the future. The other possibility, far less likely to happen, is a dramatic extension of the lifespan. The noted British expert on aging, Dr. Alex Comfort, foresees humans in the future living as long as, or longer than, biblical patriarchs. According to Comfort, half could reach 800 to 900 years—the other half might live to be 1,500! Such longevity would of course result in great overpopulation, unless balanced by an appreciable reduction from some other cause.

## PREDICTING POPULATION

Many "experts" have been embarrassed by their predictions of future population. Some years ago the president of the American Economic Association, an organization considered very knowledgeable of such trends, predicted a 10-year increase in population of about 5 million. The actual increase was closer to 20 million! In 1939, the former president of the Population Association, Henry Pratt Fairchild, suggested that if the birth rate continued to decline as it had since 1900, "by about the year 1975 there would be no babies at all!" There were babies in 1975, of course, and the population had grown from about 130 million in 1939 to 213 million.

For all its sophisticated statistical methods, even the Bureau of the Census still finds predictions of population very tricky. Today, for example, it would seem tempting to forecast a fairly rapid stabilization of population, or even a decline in the years ahead. The temptation must be resisted, however. As noted earlier, the Bureau predicted in 1943 that by about 1980 the population would have stabilized at about 153 million, obviously about 70 million too few, since by 1978 there were already nearly 218 million. Not profiting from this lesson, Professor Frank Notestein, president of the Population Council, and described as the "dean of American demographers," predicted in 1950 that for the next fifty years population growth in industrialized nations like the United States would be less than half of one percent a year. Actual growth thus far has been much more than that.

There is a parallel between weather predicting and population

128

predicting: both are moving away from actual predictions. In weather, the statistical approach has been adopted, in which we are told there is a 30-percent, or some other percent chance for rain or whatever weather seems in store. Weathermen have learned to qualify their forecasts, and the same approach has developed in population work. Past and present populations are estimated, and "projections" rather than predictions are made. Some speak of population "forecasts," but most tables presented are projections based on certain assumptions.

*Charts showing that, although our population has increased enormously since 1790, the percentage of increase has gone steadily down.*

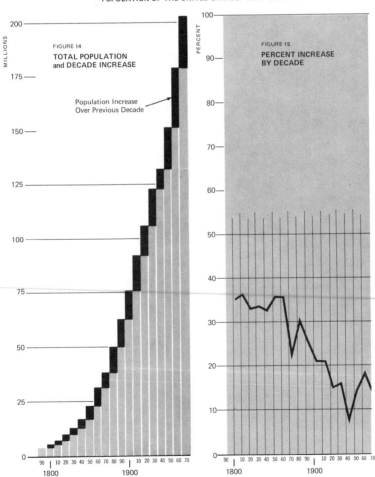

POPULATION OF THE UNITED STATES: 1790 - 1970

Although the Bureau has been wide of the mark with long-range projections in the past, it can do a good job for a few years or even a decade ahead. For example, the actual population count in 1960 was only 0.05 percent below the Bureau's estimate. In 1967 the Bureau published this series of projections for population:

|  | *1985* | *2015* |
| --- | --- | --- |
| Series A | 274,748,000 | 483,371,000 |
| Series B | 264,607,000 | 431,495,000 |
| Series C | 252,871,000 | 374,800,000 |
| Series D | 241,731,000 | 325,785,000 |

The large spread of 158 million for the year 2015 is because of the different assumptions governing the projections. Series A used the high-fertility birth rates of post World War II. Series B scaled down the fertility rates moderately, Series C still further. Series D used the lowest recorded level of fertility, excluding the Depression years.

In 1977, a new series of population projections through 2025 was made by the Bureau, using only three ranges. Surprisingly, the Series III projections for the year 2025 are considerably lower than the earlier Series A projections for 1985!

| *Year* | *Series I* | *Series II* | *Series III* |
| --- | --- | --- | --- |
| 1980 | 224 million | 222 million | 221 million |
| 1985 | 239 million | 233 million | 229 million |
| 1995 | 269 million | 253 million | 242 million |
| 2005 | 298 million | 268 million | 249 million |
| 2015 | 335 million | 283 million | 253 million |
| 2025 | 373 million | 296 million | 252 million |

Fertility assumptions vary widely in the Bureau's 1977 projections; those for mortality are the same for all series, as are immigration allowances. Even with highly sophisticated techniques, there are too many variables for accuracy more than a few years into the future. Social changes of the kind that have occurred in the past decade are an example. So is technological change, as in birth control. Economics plays a part and so do environmental conditions, disease, and other factors. The effects of immigration are unclear, as it is unknown today how many *illegal* aliens are in the United States (some estimates are as high as 8 million). Future changes in immigration laws, or of economic conditions in adjacent countries, may increase or decrease immigration. An example of this is the number of displaced people from Vietnam who are seeking a home in the United States.

## CAN POPULATION EXPLODE?

The size of America's future population is vitally important, of course. There are those who believe in and work for a reduction in growth rates, and even the achievement of zero population growth. A stabilization of population at someone's "ideal" figure might or might not work wonders on our future. Thus it is comforting to know that some authorities are confident that our country could sustain a population of as much as one billion. This would result in an average population density of only about 250 people per square mile, a level already attained or exceeded in many states and in some nations. Not everyone is so optimistic, however.

In 1960, three American scientists writing in the journal *Science* predicted that on November 13, 2026, world population would reach 50 billion. The population density at that time would be 10,000 per square mile, prompting the authors to label the date "Doomsday." That density, by the way, is somewhat less than the present density of Washington, D.C.

The Doomsday writers were following the tradition begun by the British cleric Thomas Malthus, who in 1798 published his *Essay on Population*. This treatise claimed that since the population was increasing far faster than the food supply, the world was doomed to terrible overpopulation. Malthus had access to the 1790 American census, of course, and it helped make his argument at the time. We are still feeding Americans, and a good bit of the rest of the world, and managing to take land out of cultivation each year. This does not mean that Malthus was wrong, however. Perhaps just premature!

The average worldwide birthrate in recent years has been about 34 per thousand, with a death rate of about 14. This has resulted in a population increase worldwide of about 2 percent a year. Continued for 35 years, such an increase will double the population; after 35 more years it will be four times the original figure. This is not enough to reach 50 billion by 2026, and the Doomsday trio expected an increase of about 5 percent annually. There are some examples of this. For example, the sheikhdom of Kuwait (one of the richest nations in the world because of its oil exports), has the very high birth rate of 47 per thousand. Coupled with a death rate of only 6, Kuwait is experiencing a population increase exceeding 8 percent a year, which would lead to a doubling in about 9 years. Such an increase worldwide is frightening to consider—it would produce almost 400 billion humans by the year 2026!

Moses conducted the "shekel censuses" long ago, but there were no accurate counts of *world* population until long after that. Researchers estimate that by about A.D. 1650, there may have been about half a billion humans on earth, with a very slow rise in population until that time. In just the next two centuries, population doubled to about 1 billion. After 1850, the next doubling took only 80 years. We have now reached a further doubling to 4 billion in world population. The *daily* increase in world population is about 200,000; 365 days adds 73 million more humans, and estimates are that there will be 7 billion of us in 2000. Whether or not we have a real population problem, it cannot be denied that we have *more* population all the time, with no end to the increase presently in sight. There must be a limit.

Considering America by itself, a tremendous population increase has taken place since the colonists settled here. It is estimated that when Columbus reached the New World, there were perhaps 1 million Indians living in all of North America. Three hundred years later, the first American census showed about 4 million people in the tiny United States alone. For 70 years after that our population increased about 35 percent each decade. It dropped to less than 20 percent in the 1860 census, and further declined so that now it increases less than 1 percent a year. Even 1 percent a year will double our population in 70 years, however, and a doubling of population is something to be considered carefully and planned for as well.

# THE CONTROL OF POPULATION

Many people since Thomas Malthus have been concerned about overpopulation. In recent years there has been more said about that problem, and for a while the talking bordered on panic. The American political establishment paid scant attention, however, and as late at 1960 President Eisenhower stated that he "could not imagine anything more emphatically not a proper political or governmental activity, function, or responsibility, than population control."

In 1963 President Kennedy, a Roman Catholic with a heritage of large families, had the courage to warn the Central American countries that if we did not stem the human tide, we would all be inundated in an immense ocean of poverty. Although Kennedy took no concrete action on his philosophy, his successor did. President Johnson in December of 1967 signed a United Nations "Declaration on World Population," which said in part:

> It took mankind all of recorded time until the middle of the last century to achieve a population of one billion. Yet it took less than a hundred years to add the second billion and only thirty years to add the third. At today's rate of increase, there will be four billion people by 1975 and nearly seven billion by the year 2000. This unprecedented increase presents us with a situation unique in human affairs and a problem that grows more urgent with each passing day.

Matching action to these noble words, Johnson set up a blue-ribbon committee of experts as a Committee on Population and Family Planning, chaired by John D. Rockefeller III, an acknowledged expert in the field of population. It was President Nixon who received the Committee's report urging the formation of a formal Population Committee. Nixon pointed out that "many of our present social problems may be related to the fact that we have had only fifty years in which to accommodate the second hundred million Americans." In March of 1970 he signed a bill setting up the Commission on Population Growth and gave the Commission a tough list of responsibilities:

Determine the probable course of U.S. population growth and internal migration.

Estimate the resources needed to deal with anticipated population growth.

Project the impact of population growth on federal and state governments.

Survey the effects of population growth on environmental pollution and the depletion of natural resources.

Seek ways of achieving a population level commensurate with the ethical values and resources of the United States.

In its 1972 report to the White House, the Population Commission said:

We have always assumed that progress and the "good life" are connected with population growth. In fact, population growth has frequently been regarded as a measure of our progress. If that was ever the case, it is not now. There is hardly any social problem confronting our nation whose solution would be easier if our population were larger.

It is a remarkable fact that in December of that same year an American birth rate less than that required for long-term maintenance of population was discovered by the Bureau of the Census. (Japan had already achieved this birth rate in 1957.)

What had happened was that enough women had put off having children so that the average rate of babies produced during the lifetime of a woman was only about 1.8. And that number is just not enough to maintain the population at its present level.

It was as though our race consciousness, or our subconscious, had somehow become aware of the Population Commission warning and had taken action in the most direct way possible. Not much came out of the Population Commission after that—perhaps its deliberations were unnecessary in the face of what seemed like zero population growth as accomplished fact.

Within the overall population increases in our nation are interesting differences in various ethnic groups. The chapter on

134

People notes the very rapid increase in Indian population, for example. There has been an even more dramatic increase in what are sometimes called "pockets of fertility," such as the Hutterite culture. These people increased their numbers from about 8,500 to 16,000 in the 15 years between 1950 to 1965, several times as great an increase as the population as a whole. The Amish people also have shown a rapid increase in population, particularly in the case of Mr. and Mrs. John Miller, who had a total of 410 descendants before Miller died at age 95!

It is tempting, but ridiculous, to base population predictions on such statistics. For example, some misguided seers pointed with alarm to the fact that if the Hutterites continued to increase as they had up to 1965, there would be 55 million of them in a century. In two centuries they would number in the billions! Such projections hardly ever come about because balancing forces sooner or later slow down such population spurts.

There is very little danger that the Indians, the Hutterites, or any other ethnic group will take over the world or even the United States. Of much greater concern is the continuing trend for the less-developed nations to increase population much more rapidly than those more developed. In India, for example, people expect their children to take care of them in their old age, and since there is such a high mortality rate of infants, they need a lot of children to be sure some will survive them. Thus it is hard to convince them of the merits of birth control.

What is not yet clear is what will happen to the balance of power with some nations maintaining a zero-population-growth policy while others continue to grow at present rates. For example, a century from now there could be several supernations with populations higher than 1.5 billion. Mexico and Brazil would qualify at that figure, and India would have a population of 9 billion souls—25 to 30 times that of the United States! At the same time China will have grown to about 6 billion, 1½ times the present population of the entire world. China presently could lose half its people in a war and still have a formidable population.

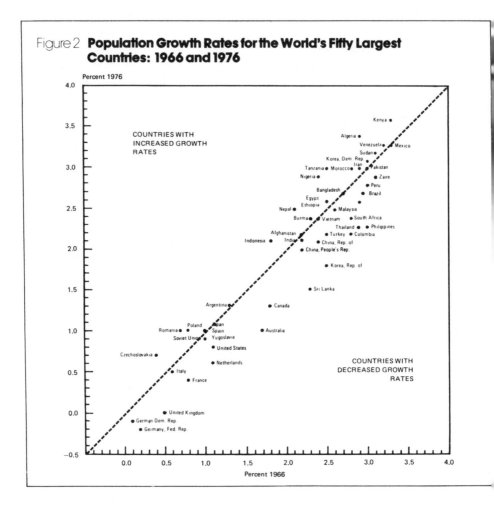

Figure 2 **Population Growth Rates for the World's Fifty Largest Countries: 1966 and 1976**

Percent 1976

COUNTRIES WITH
INCREASED GROWTH
RATES

Kenya ●

Algeria ●

Venezuela ●  ● Mexico
Sudan ●
Korea, Dem. Rep. ●
Iran
Tanzania ● Morocco ●  ● ● Pakistan
Nigeria ●  ● Zaire
● Peru
Bangladesh ●  ● Brazil
Egypt ●
Nepal ●  Ethiopia ●  ● Malaysia
Burma ●  ● Vietnam  ● South Africa
Thailand ●  ● Philippines
Afghanistan ●  ● Turkey  ● Colombia
Indonesia ●  India ●  ● China, Rep. of
● China, People's Rep.

● Korea, Rep. of

● Sri Lanka

Argentina ●  ● Canada

Poland
Romania ●  ● ● Japan
● Spain  ● Australia
Soviet Union ●  Yugoslavia ●
Czechoslovakia ●  ● United States
● Netherlands
● Italy  COUNTRIES WITH
DECREASED GROWTH
● France  RATES

● United Kingdom
● German Dem. Rep.
● Germany, Fed. Rep.

Percent 1966

*Fast as the American population has been expanding, we still belong among those developed countries whose rate of growth has decreased.*

## SUMMARY

The present American generation coexists with twice as many Americans as did the last generation, and with more than fifty times as many as the generation who responded to the 1790 census. Are we better off for that, or worse? Those who ponder this question undoubtedly have many different views, and it would be difficult to say which is the proper view. Future population in America in all

136

probability will be determined not by a Population Commission, a dictator, or a planning computer. It will result from a variety of factors, including our economic welfare, wars or their lack, the American life-style, and perhaps the weather and other environmental forces. For a while, at least, we seem sure to grow in numbers. The census will continue to measure that growth, and also to provide us with facts and figures for better handling our increasing population.

# 8
# Confidentiality

The sole purpose of the census is to acquire general statistical information regarding the population and resources of the country, and replies are required from individuals only in order to permit the compilation of such general statistics. The census has nothing to do with taxation, with army or jury service, with the compulsion of school attendance, with the regulation of immigration, or with the enforcement of any national, State, or local law or ordinance, nor can any person be harmed in any way by furnishing the information required. There need be no fear that any disclosure will be made regarding any individual person or his affairs. For the due protection of the rights and interests of the persons furnishing information, every employee of the Census Bureau is prohibited, under heavy penalty, from disclosing any information which may thus come to his knowledge.
—*President William Howard Taft*

In 1980 you are required to respond to the Census of Population and Housing with a great deal of personal information, particularly if you are one of those receiving the expanded questionnaires sent to 22 percent of the population. Here are some of those questions you may be required by law to answer:

Educational attainment
Ancestry
Current language
Presence of disability or handicap
Date of first marriage and whether terminated by death
Employment status
Whether looking for work

Your housing questionnaire may ask the following:

Year built
Method of sewage disposal

Number of bathrooms
Existence of specific structural deficiencies or damage
Homeowner shelter costs for mortgages, real estate taxes, and
hazard insurance
Existence of property improvement

Most of us have little hesitation about answering such questions, but most probably prefer that the information be kept confidential. Assuming that you do not want this information made available to anyone who might use it to your harm, can you be sure this will not happen? The Bureau of the Census has gone to great lengths to safeguard what it considers a sacred trust. Printed on your questionnaire is this promise:

Your answers are CONFIDENTIAL. The law requires that you answer the questions to the best of your knowledge. Your answers will be used only for statistical purposes and cannot, by law, be disclosed to any person outside the Census Bureau for any reason whatsoever.

Behind this promise is 190 years of establishing the guarantee for such a safeguard.

## HISTORY

We have noted that historically many people have objected to being counted and questioned in censuses. Religious concern was one common reason, but there were many others. Leading figures in England and Europe branded the enumeration of people and property "a scandalous invasion of privacy." Yet, surprisingly, when America instituted its countrywide census in 1790, not only did federal marshals count heads and collect other facts from each household, they were also required by law to post copies of the findings thus gathered at "two of the most public places in their respective districts, there to remain for the inspection of all concerned." Hardly a comforting precedent for confidentiality!

It may seem remarkable that there was no revolt against this first censual invasion of American privacy. However, the facts collected and so publicly displayed were most likely known by just about everyone before being spotlighted in the town square. Unlike the Colonial censuses, those of 1790 and 1800 recorded only names of heads of families, number of free persons by age and sex, and the number of slaves in each family.

By 1810, however, census questions began to grow in number and inquisitiveness. The motive was generally good: to learn how healthy the new nation was, how many citizens were literate, how many had served in the military (the original reason for the biblical census and other early ones), plus token information on manufacturing, trade, crop production, and so on. For all its good intentions, however, this development in census taking brought vocal objections from many. This included businessmen, who saw the questions as attempts to tax them more and at the same time broadcast their trade secrets. In response to this outcry, each federal marshal and assistant in 1840 was told for the first time "to consider all communications made to him in the performance of his duty, relative to the business of the people, as strictly confidential."

As the lists of questions grew longer and more prying, marshals were given further warnings about the confidentiality of the information they were gathering. Specifically, they were "expected to consider the facts intrusted to them as if obtained exclusively for the use of the Government, and not to be used in any way to the gratification of curiosity, the exposure of any man's business or pursuits, or for their private emolument, who, while employed in this service, act as agents of the Government in the most confidential capacity." In other words, no stealing of secrets or taking bribes for so doing.

In 1850 each free person was required to have his name recorded, together with specified details in a number of areas. Slaves were to be personally identified, and certain data also recorded about each. Farmers, manufacturers, miners, and tradesmen were required to describe more details of their operations. It was thus a blessing that with the 1850 census the posting of the actual forms in public places was discontinued, for the questions asked were revelations not many wanted posted for public inspection.

In 1870 categories and questions about slaves no longer existed, of course, and the question framers shifted their attention to other areas. The Congressional inquisition included questions not only about wealth but also debts. Amounts of wages, prices, and taxes were required, along with information on insurance. Crimes were recorded, along with pauperism, physical and mental shortcomings, and religious beliefs.

For several censuses, marshals had been instructed to safeguard the confidentiality of census information. How well this was done is a matter of question, since everything was left to the moral judgment of men paid poorly for a thankless task. The Tenth Census Act, which provided for the 1880 Census, was the first to contain a *legal* ban on the disclosure of census information. By now, civilian supervisors and enumerators had replaced the marshals and their assistants. Each of these new civil servants was required to swear "not to disclose any information contained in the schedule, lists, or statements obtained by me to any person or persons, except to my superior officers." The new law had teeth in it, too: conviction of a violation of this trust carried with it a fine of up to $500! And in 1880 that sum was enough to make a tempted officer think very carefully of the risk.

Another safeguard to privacy was instituted at the same time. Until then it had been the practice to retain original census schedules in the local area, but in 1880 these were sent to Washington. Only name, age, sex and race were filed locally. This must have been a relief to Americans, because by 1890 not just six questions were asked but 470! And many of them were drafted not by census officials but by Congress itself.

The all-time low in census prying came in 1880 and 1890. Southern reconstruction was faltering, and racism was strong in the Congress and in the Supreme Court as well. The census-form question about race required not just a response of white or Negro, but all the many shades between; specifically, the census asked if a person was Negro, mulatto, quadroon, or octaroon. The enumerator's guidebook in 1880 contained this instruction: "Be particularly careful in reporting the class *mulatto*. The word here is generic, and includes all persons having any perceptible trace of African blood. Important scientific results depend on the correct determination of this class."

Not only race but physical differences and mental problems were

141

of almost morbid interest to the framers of census questions. Here are samples:

*About physical oddities:* "Whether the person, being 20 years of age or over, is less than 4 feet 1 inch or over 6 feet 8 inches high; if so, give height in feet and inches."
*About homeless children:* "Has the origin of this child been respectable? . . . Is he (or she) an idiot?"
*About paupers and "benevolence":* "Is he (or she) habitually intemperate? A 'tramp?' 'Syphilitic?' An 'habitual drunkard?' 'Insane?' 'Idiotic?' "
*About the insane:* "Does this person require to be usually or often restrained by any mechanical appliance, such as a strap, straitjacket, etc.? . . . If married, inquire whether wife or husband of this person is insane, blind, deaf, or deformed from infancy."
*About idiots:* "Head size (large, small, or natural)? Age at which idiocy occurred?"

Such census questions are little comfort to those who fear the intrusion of government into the private affairs of its citizens. For whatever reasons, congressmen a century ago framed questions today considered vicious. In the name of "scientific inquiry," the census reflected racism and a prying concern with biological and social differences.

By 1890 not even brief lists of persons enumerated were filed in the local courts. A municipal government could obtain such lists only by requesting them from the Bureau of the Census. However, though "secrets" were safeguarded locally, the slow change of procedure moved those same secrets to a central location within the federal government. In time this development set off the fear in some Americans that they had slipped from the frying pan into the fire. As government grew in size and power, citizens began to fear a "Big Brother" able to spy on them from a central site to which all information was channeled under penalty of law. It was bad enough to have local or state authorities privy to one's secrets, but to know that such information was available to the federal government frightened some people far more, even with the assurance that the information would not be used for purposes of taxation, regulation, or investigation.

With the creation of the Bureau of the Census in 1902, census taking became a more professional operation. Continuity was achieved when the same employees were involved in successive censuses. And attempts were made in 1910 to further guarantee confidentiality for citizens required to tell more and more to enumerators. The $500 fine for employees of the Bureau of the Census who violated confidentiality was raised to $1,000, or imprisonment for up to two years, or both. Penalties in force today are greater.

In the area of personal information, the Director of the Census was given the discretion to release to governors and local courts of record certified copies of statistical totals for states or jurisdictions, respectively. Another power given the Director was that of furnishing to individuals "such data from the population schedules as may be desired for genealogical or other proper purposes." The right of states and courts to census information was limited in 1920 census legislation: "In no case shall the information furnished be used to the detriment of the person or persons to whom such information relates." In 1923, however, the names and addresses of illiterates were still being furnished to some states.

The census inquisition abated in 1930, when the Census Bureau itself began to write the questions asked in the schedules. It has continued to do this task, and recently has set up pre-census conferences to seek the help of those to be counted. Its aim now is to gather the greatest amount of information without offending the sensitivities of those who must respond to census questionnaires.

The 1940 census asked a question on income; persons earning more than $5,000 were requested to indicate so on the form. Among those objecting was United States Senator Charles Tobey (Rep., New Hampshire) who called the question unconstitutional and in violation of the Bill of Rights. Tobey's battle cry was "Eternal vigilance is still the price of liberty. Stand up and fight!" Many individuals and organizations agreed, and a campaign was launched to prevent the inclusion of the income question. The Bureau compromised by including a separate form to be mailed directly to Washington; however, only about 2 percent of the total questioned used them.

Prior to the 1970 census there was a more serious confidentiality controversy, generally thought to have been inspired by earlier proposals for a National Data Bank that would consolidate all sorts of information about Americans and make it accessible through a single identification, such as the social security number. This time Congressman Jackson E. Betts launched a campaign to limit drastically the questions on the 1970 census, and many groups joined the effort. Betts argued for making all but seven questions *voluntary*. Arguments against "prying questions" on the census included cartoons asking "With whom do you share your shower?" The American Civil Liberties Union got involved, but accepted every question except that concerning race. After all the argument, the response to the 1970 census was excellent, and returns came in even faster than had been expected. The response was thought by the Bureau Director to have been better than in 1960.

To sum up the history of census confidentiality in the field: from the first census in 1790 to 1830, there was none. From 1840 to 1870 there were still no *legal* restrictions concerning census information, but field personnel were required to take an oath not to disclose any census information; violation of this trust could result in a fine of $500.

Since 1910 only sworn census employees in census headquarters may examine an individual census report, and data can be used only for statistical purposes. Law prohibits the publication of any information that might identity an individual. Confidentiality applies to the 10-year censuses of population and housing, the 5-year censuses of agriculture, business, manufactures, mineral industries, construction, and transportation, as well as the great number of annual, quarterly, monthly, and weekly surveys.

## OUR CENSUS RESPONSIBILITY

The census in America is not voluntary, we are *required* to answer questions asked in the census. In 1790, any individual refusing to answer could be fined $20, a sizable sum then. In time this grew to as much as a $10,000 fine and jail terms ranging from sixty days to one year. Chapter 7 of Title 13 of the U.S. Code covers Offenses and Penalties. There are two sections, one pertaining to officers and employees of the Bureau of the Census, and one to "other persons." For making "false statements, certificates, and information," an officer or employee of the Bureau is subject to a fine of not more than $2,000, or imprisonment of not more than five years, or both. For "wrongful disclosure of census information," such a person is subject to a fine of not more than $5,000, imprisonment of not more than five years, or both.

For "refusal or neglect to answer questions, or false answers," any person over 18 years of age is subject to a fine of no more than $100. For a willfully false answer the fine is a maximum of $500. However, no person is compelled to answer any question about religious belief or church membership.

For "giving suggestions or information with intent to cause inaccurate enumeration of population," a person is subject to a fine of not more than $1,000, imprisonment of not more than one year, or both.

For "refusal by owners, proprietors, etc., to assist census employees," a person is subject to a fine of not more than $500. For "failure to answer questions affecting companies, businesses, religious bodies, and other organizations; false answers," a person is subject to a fine of not more than $500. For willfully giving a false answer concerning a business or other organization, the fine shall be no more than $10,000.

No one has ever paid such a stiff fine for refusal to answer census questions. Individuals have refused, however, and been fined small amounts.

## HOW IS CONFIDENTIALITY PRESERVED?

This is the sixty-four-dollar question. It would, of course, be possible for *someone* to get confidential information about you. After all, census employees handle our questionnaires and check them, and data-processing technicians also handle questionnaires containing names and addresses. However, these employees have taken an oath to safeguard confidential census information and can pay stiff penalties for failing to observe that oath. It is also difficult to imagine why anyone would go to the lengths required to learn from the census that you suffer from rheumatoid arthritis; it is so much simpler to check you out in person!

Assuming that all steps are carried out properly, confidentiality can be maintained while important statistical information is used. After you, or a census taker, has marked your questionnaire and that document has been delivered for processing, no name, address, or other information is given to the computer. As a result, no person, no family, no housing unit can be specifically identified in the resulting statistical output. Information is there to be used by whoever has use for it, but no one will know any particulars about individuals. Unless someone—a Census employee or other person—breaks a law and releases such personal information, no one can know that *you* earned $17,890 last year, that *you* were a high-school dropout, that *you* have been married twice (or not at all), or that *you* have six children, one of whom is adopted.

In effect, although you pour out a great deal of personal and business information, as far as the Bureau's computer is concerned, you remain a nameless, faceless statistic from which it can only produce facts and figures. Dr. A. Ross Eckler, Director of the Census Bureau from 1965 through 1969, told a congressional committee that never, since confidentiality laws were passed, has this trust been breached. Directors before and since, as well as United States Presidents, have said the same thing, with apparent confidence.

The Bureau provides two-fold protection for respondents to census questionnaires. First, questions are carefully screened for "need and appropriateness." Answers are then so handled that Census Bureau records reveal no individual information about persons, families, or businesses. This is guaranteed because the high-speed cameras that convert census questionnaires to tiny microfilms never see your name or address.

There is no end to the nosy questions that individuals and groups can think up. Prior to the 1940 census, for example, more than 6,000 suggested questions came in to the Bureau. These ranged from ownership of burial plots to belief in God and color of hair (desired by cosmetics manufacturers). Almost all were turned down. More recent questions have included:

Do you own a cat?

Do you own a bird?

Do you smoke cigarettes? Cigars? When did you begin smoking?

Do you belong to a union? Which one?

Have you ever been in an automobile accident?

What is your overall tax bill?

Do you own a piano? An organ? A violin? Other musical instrument?

The Bureau rejects thousands of questions on two grounds: first, no question is included unless there is an important need by a public agency for answers to it; second, every question must be readily answerable by the average person.

## FOUR LEVELS OF PROTECTION

Once you have provided information on the census questionnaire, there are four levels at which that information must be safeguarded if true confidentiality is to be maintained. These four levels are: in the field during the taking of the census; in census headquarters during the processing of the data; in published statistical tabulations; and finally, in the records themselves stored for safekeeping. Here is how the Bureau ensures confidentiality at all four levels:

*In the Field.* Since 1880, all field personnel have been required by law to take an oath not to disclose any information collected, and they are subject to stiff penalties for violation.

*In Census Headquarters.* Since 1900, all employees in census headquarters have been required to take the oath of confidentiality, subject to the penalties existing for other employees. Since 1910, no one other than a sworn census employee can examine the individual reports.

*Publication of Statistical Tabulations.* Since 1910, law has prohibited the publication of statistical information whereby a business or industrial establishment may be identified. In 1930 that law was extended to cover individuals from such identification.

*Stored Records.* Under present law (Title 13), all records since 1900 are "Census Confidential," and the Bureau of the Census is legally prohibited from disclosing information in the records except as statistical totals or in the form of a certificate conveying a person's own record to him or his authorized legal representative upon his signed application.

A visitor to the Bureau of the Census in Suitland or elsewhere sees firsthand how sensitive the Bureau is to preserving the confidentiality of material in its trust. To visit sensitive areas one must gain permission of the Public Information Office and the heads of the respective sections. Next the visitor is required to fill out a form and wear a special badge in plain sight during the entire visit. And a Census Bureau official accompanies him or her every step of the way.

## ALTERNATIVES

It has been suggested that the Bureau guard the privacy of individuals by having name-and-address information on a "tear-off" section of the census questionnaire. After processing, this personal information would be removed and destroyed. Unfortunately, such safeguards of individual privacy would "throw the baby out with the bath water" and make it impossible later to locate personal information to help an individual needing a passport, proof of birth, or other information his census records could provide.

Another approach to confidentiality would be to make the answering of all questions voluntary, rather than mandatory. Each respondent could decide what not to tell. When this philosophy was urged before the 1970 census, Arthur C. Nielsen, Jr., president of the marketing research company, spoke strongly for mandatory censuses. Nielsen called voluntary census cooperation a wolf in sheep's clothing and a real threat to the historic validity of the census. Without knowledge of the "universe" reported by the census, strong bias can enter the results, making them far less valid than a mandatory response—which has historically reflected about 97.5 percent of the population. Neilsen compared the census with mandatory speed limits, that operate for the safety of not just the motorist complying but for all of us as well. Similarly, we have mandatory regulations and restrictions concerning sewer lines, utilities, and pollution.

## LAW SUITS

There are several types of legal problems involving the census. The first is that of an individual who refuses to answer questions as required by law. The second problem is that of a Census Bureau employee who violates his oath to keep confidential all census material so protected. Third is an individual, business, or other entity which feels that its rights to privacy have been violated. A fourth case, which until recently had not been a problem, involves foreign trade. Although there have been test cases in all these areas, their scarcity suggests little problem in the past with confidentiality of Census records. At the same time, some recent lawsuits have raised questions that may pose problems.

In all the years since confidentiality was established and penalties fixed for violations of the law by Census employees, there has been only one such case. During the census of 1900, Joseph Moriarity, a special agent of the Census Office, was indicted for making a false, fictitious, and fraudulent return on Census of Manufactures schedule. Specifically, Moriarity made up a schedule for a nonexistent firm. During the trial, he admitted all the charges against him, but contended that his acts did not violate the law because the Census Act of 1900 was unconstitutional.

On February 20, 1901, District Court Judge Edward B. Thomas, of the U.S. District Court, 2nd Circuit, Southern District of New York, found Moriarity guilty as charged. His decision said in part, "The functions vested in the National Government authorize the obtainment of the information demanded in sections of the Census Act, and the exercise of the right befits an exalted and progressive sovereign power, enacting laws adopted to the needs of the vast and varied interests of the people, after acquiring detailed knowledge thereof. . . ."

Only two Americans have been brought to trial for failure to answer questions on the census form. Better known is the case of

William F. Rickenbacker of New York, son of the noted flier Eddy
Rickenbacker. In 1962, the younger Rickenbacker was convicted in
U.S. District Court for the Southern District of New York (the
same court that had heard Moriarity's case). He had received a
sample household questionnaire sent to every fourth household,
but told the census enumerator he would not answer the questions.
He later told the Grand Jury that indicted him that his refusal was
based upon the belief that the questionnaire was "an unnecessary
invasion of my privacy," and upon his desire "to maintain liberties
in this country as a constitutional philosophical question." Rickenbacker was given a suspended sentence of sixty days, fined $100,
and placed on probation for one day. He later appealed the sentence, but the Circuit Court upheld the conviction.

A similar case in 1970 resulted in the sentencing of Thomas
Little, for failure to answer census questions. The decision read in
part, "The authority to gather reliable statistical data reasonably
related to governmental purposes and functions is a necessity if
modern government is to legislate intelligently and effectively."

It is understandable that many government agencies desire the
personal data tucked away in the information gathered by the
Bureau of the Census. For example, in 1930, the Women's Bureau
of the U.S. Department of Labor asked for the names and addresses
of women working in Rochester, New York. The Bureau of the
Census refused, and in the resulting legal action, the United States
Attorney General upheld the Bureau's action.

The most heart-warming example of the confidentiality maintained occurred on the West Coast after the Japanese bombing of
Pearl Harbor in World War II. When the War Department decided to imprison Japanese-Americans, it went to the Bureau of the
Census for their names and addresses, which the Bureau had, of
course. The War Department had good precedent. For example,
Social Security information (which we were promised would be
kept secret) is routinely given to the FBI, the Secret Service, the
Immigration and Naturalization Service, as well as welfare agencies
of the various states. By law, your federal tax returns also can be
studied by the FBI, and by agents of Narcotics, Customs, and the
Secret Service. Faced with the demand for Japanese-American

names and addresses, however, the Bureau of the Census balked, pointing to the law against such disclosures. The refusal stood, and the War Department received only geographical data from which the military had to select likely neighborhoods for those they sought.

The Immigration and Naturalization Service, knowing of the gold mines of data in Census records, some years ago asked for the addresses of persons it wanted to deport. But the Bureau of Census refused, and again the Justice Department backed them up. Representative Cornelius Gallagher (Dem., New Jersey), chairman of a House subcommittee investigating government agencies collecting private information, reported in 1971 that there was evidence of leaks everywhere but from the Bureau of the Census. A later Senate investigation led by Senator Sam Ervin required little time to decide that risks of disclosure were minor. And Representative Jackson Betts (Rep., Ohio), a strong critic of the how-many-people-use-the-same-bathtub-type question in the census, admitted, "I can't recall even any hint that the Census information was leaking out in any form."

When the White House was being restored some years ago, the Census Bureau refused the Administration a list of persons living in an exclusive Washington suburb so that living quarters for the President could be found! About the closest thing to a charge of illegal disclosure by a Census employee in recent times was the claim in 1970 by a woman living in Washington, D.C., that a census taker had leaked her telephone number to a "criss-cross" directory. However, an investigation disclosed that the number was more probably acquired by the directory in some other manner.

Most lawsuits filed having to do with census confidentiality concern demands for business information. There have been a fair number of such suits, but in only one did the courts rule in favor of releasing census information, and that situation was quickly corrected by Congress. The following are cases most frequently cited.

In 1960, Beatrice Foods Company of Chicago was ordered to provide to the Federal Trade Commission its file copies of census schedules submitted to the Bureau of the Census in 1954. A U.S. Court of Appeals ruled in favor of the company, but the U.S.

Supreme Court ordered Beatrice Foods to comply with the FTC request. Shortly thereafter, the Bureau of the Census asked Congress to pass legislation giving file copies of census documents confidential status. Congress complied quickly, and since that time no census confidentiality suit has been lost.

Subsequent cases include those of the St. Regis Paper Company, involving demands for census documents for use in a suit concerning pollution; Becton, Dickinson and Company, a drug firm charged with monopolizing the hypodermic syringe market; the Seymour v. Barraba case, in which demands for the records of sugar companies were made of the then director of the Census Bureau; the American Jewish Congress boycott case involving a demand for Commerce Secretary Thurston B. Morton to name the firms in that boycott; and the United States v. International Business Machines Corporation, an antitrust action in which IBM sought the census records of other companies to defend itself.

The United States government has been on both sides of confidentiality cases, but the protection of census information has been consistently upheld, regardless of who seeks to have it released. Underlying this consistency is the basic thought expressed in this excerpt from the opinion of the court hearing the case of United States v. Bethlehem Steel Corp.:

> One need not probe far to understand that when Congress imposed upon citizens the duty of disclosing information of a confidential and intimate nature, its purpose was to protect those who complied with the command of the statute. Apart from giving assurance to citizens that the integrity of the information would be preserved by the Government, another purpose was to encourage citizens to submit freely all data desired in recognition of its importance in the enactment of laws and other purposes in the national interests.

The Bureau of the Census itself diligently goes beyond the letter of the law in protecting economic data from those who must supply it. Economic Fields Director Shirley Kallek recalls a request from an association, made up of every firm in that trade but one, for a special survey of all such firms. Realizing that by the process of elimination this would yield information about the nonmember of the association, the Bureau refused to comply with the request.

# TROUBLE AHEAD?

In 1944 the U.S. Attorney General stated:

> The Archivist of the United States is legally bound to observe the various provisions of the census laws governing the confidential treatment of census records with respect to those records which are transferred into his custody pursuant to the National Archives Act.

Although census information seems to be sacrosanct, these tight restrictions apply only to the censuses of 1910 through 1970. They do, of course, also apply to the 1980 census and the first 5-year census of population and housing in 1985. However, the public is free to inspect all other censuses (with the exception of the 1890 census, most of which was destroyed by a fire in 1921). These records are in the National Archives and Records Center in Washington, D.C., and the reason for this openness is legal: There was no confidentiality law at all from 1790 to 1870, and in 1880 and 1890 only supervisors and enumerators were bound to maintain the secrecy of collected information.

Although the law seems to protect and secure census material gathered from 1900 on, some recent developments threaten to take away this security. By law, material from census records is stored in the National Archives after a certain length of time, and the National Archives is governed not by U.S. Title 13 laws but those in Title 44. Because of this, the Archivist had the authority, and recently exercised it, to open 1900 records for the use of genealogists and others. Title 44 gives seventy-two years as the length of time for holding Archives material sacrosanct. This seems to suggest that each ten years, material from another census will be made public.

At first it seemed that in such disclosures names would not be permitted to be used, but even this safeguard has been dropped. Researchers now may publish not only census information but the name and addresses of those to whom it pertains as well. Such an approach goes far beyond the former ruling that only an individual himself could receive such information.

Genealogy, of course, makes good use of census data. (While at the Bureau's headquarters in Suitland, I took the opportunity to look through the South Carolina census reports from 1790. My hope was to find mention of my mother's family—her maiden name was Edwards. I was overly successful, for there were 48 Edwardses listed!) Such records, including family names, plus a wealth of other data about the families, are a fertile source for anyone interested in his forebears. An article in the *New York Times* shortly after the opening of the 1900 census urged Jews seeking genealogical information to visit the Census depositories near them to examine the 1900 census. It contains the names, occupation, date of birth, year of immigration, nationality of parents, year of marriage, education, and citizenship of each individual. The census may also list the names of other people living in a reporting household.

The law that permits the opening up of once confidential material after seventy-two years makes available data concerning an estimated 6 to 7 million people listed in the 1900 census records who are still alive. What effect the revelation will have on those thus exposed to public gaze will only be learned with time. For example, in the 1910 census material that probably will be opened to the public in the next decade are enumerations of "houses of ill repute," with name after name of the inmates thereof! Here are the names and addresses of prostitutes and others involved in the business, whose families would then be exposed to whatever may result from such an airing of information long pledged safe.

## FREEDOM OF INFORMATION

In recent years there have been several pieces of legislation aimed at tearing away the cloak of secrecy in a number of situations. One is popularly called the Government in the Sunshine, or just the Sunshine Act. Another is the Freedom of Information Act. A surprising result of this new legislation (and the publicity given the stripping away of the veil) is that the Foreign Trade Act has been greatly weakened. A lawsuit is pending over the request of the Twin Coast Shipping Company for complete records about certain exports and imports. This information would list all customers, goods, prices, and trade secrets, and would obviously benefit those who received it. Census officials are concerned that should Twin

Coast win this test case, it will then be impossible for the Bureau to guarantee or provide the confidentiality pledged to businesses asked to bare their records for the Census.

## THE ONE EXCEPTION:
## PERSONAL CENSUS SERVICE

Census confidentiality promises that there is only one person who can breach the wall separating your Census data from a prying outside world, and that person is *you*, or your heirs, or a legal representative, because there are times when you or these people need information that may only be available from the Bureau of the Census.

Documentary evidence is often needed for naturalization papers, passports, inheritance claims, pensions; to establish ancestry; for employment, retirement, a driver's license, voter registration, insurance, military service, income-tax matters, a marriage license, or welfare benefits. The Social Security Administration and the Railroad Retirement Board both rely on census records.

Information on minor children also may be obtained through a written request from either parent. The records of a deceased person can be obtained with an application by a blood relative in the immediate family, the surviving spouse, a beneficiary, or the administrator or executor of the estate. A death certificate is required, of course.

In 1903, Congress permitted the Bureau to set up a service for searching census records for proof of age, race, place of birth, and residence. Business was not brisk at the start, however, and in 1909 the service brought in a total of only $32. In 1913 requests began to grow, when Civil-War and Spanish-American War veterans were seeking certificates with which to apply for pensions. As a result, the Bureau had to put 28 clerks to work searching 1860 census records. Since then requests have averaged about 250,000 a year. During World War II the demand for age searches reached a total of 737,000 in a single year, as Americans needed proof of citizenship to go to work in war plants. More recently, Medicare caused business to boom at the Personal Census Service Branch.

Age searches are gradually declining, and are being exceeded by genealogical searches. Presently there are about 400 requests each week for this kind of information. Fees collected are in the range of $2 million annually and make the facility self-supporting.

The Personal Census Service Branch is headquartered in Pittsburgh, Kansas 66762, and you may mail such a request directly to that facility, or fill it out at the bureau of the Census in Suitland, Maryland, or at any of its 12 regional offices, the Department of Commerce headquarters in Washington, or some of its district offices. The charge is $8.50 for a search of two censuses and a transcript of the information found, with additional copies for $1 each. Census transcripts cannot be furnished, however, for the purpose of tracking down missing persons, beneficial as such searches may be.

## SUMMARY

The Census Bureau truly seems caught between a rock and a hard place. On one hand, it must ask for a great deal of information from us as individuals and businessmen. On the other, it must guarantee us that such information will never be used to our harm. Up to now, the Bureau has done an excellent job of walking this statistical tightrope. Charges that it pries into our personal affairs and allows that information to be available to others outside the Bureau have not been documented. Indeed, the Bureau has bent backward in safeguarding our confidentiality.

What lies in the future is unclear. Pressed by business for more specific information, and by laws ordering the freedom of information involving information previously treated as secret, the Bureau may have a difficult time in complying without violating its traditional confidentiality. Accomplishing its mission has never been easy; in the years ahead the task seems destined to be more difficult than ever.

# 9
# The Census Takers

One of every thousand Americans served in 1970 as a census-taker.

*E.J. Kahn, Jr.*

About 12,000 employees work for the Bureau of the Census on a permanent or continuing part-time basis. But by far the greatest number of census workers serve the country only once every ten years, and then for only a few weeks or months. For the 1980 census a real "army" has been recruited, trained, and used as enumerators, clerks, and other workers. This army consists of a quarter-million men and women, equivalent to two thirds the population of Alaska.

Census enumerators have included schoolteachers, college professors, students, ministers, a 101-year-old Death Valley prospector, an admiral, the warden of Sing Sing Prison, and Bureau of the Census professionals. Schoolteachers have a long history of census taking. Recently, American teachers covered the remote areas of Alaska; foreign teachers have done census work around the world in places like prewar Hungary, and more recently the African Sudan. In China, missionaries served for a long time as census takers.

Census takers cover not just private homes and apartments.

157

*Counting frozen noses in Alaska—near Fairbanks, an enumerator takes down facts for completing the 1940 census.*

They also visit hotels, motels, houseboats, missions, flophouses, orphanages, hospitals, and prisons. Some scour the banks of rivers, peer under bridges, and comb the steam tunnels under New York City. Chicken houses, boxcars, abandoned buses and trolleys, crates and caves are fair game too. Enumerators have surprised thieves in people's homes, and counted heads in "houses of ill fame." In the latter case they see and hear no evil because of the strict confidentiality laws that protect a respondent's privacy.

In the Florida Everglades census takers set up shop in stores and take the census as swamp residents come to buy supplies. Those who don't come in must be reached by shallow-draft "air boats." A special problem some enumerators have is convincing moonshiners they are from the Census Bureau and not the Treasury Department. Census takers make their rounds on foot or horseback, on snowshoes or skis, in cars, outrigger canoes, airplanes, helicopters, snowcats, dogsleds, motorboats, and rowboats. At times they find

*A conscientious census taker doesn't let remoteness stop him from reaching every countable American.*

themselves in the middle of family arguments or other emergencies. They have delivered babies, washed diapers, taken in the wash, and fought fires.

The Postal Service is proud that "neither snow nor rain nor heat, nor gloom of night stays these couriers from the swift completion of their appointed rounds." Census takers are of the same breed. In New Hampshire, one rode up Mount Washington in a snowstorm, clinging to the side of a snowcat. The wind was blowing at 70 miles an hour, and he could see only 5 feet ahead, but he got to the top and interviewed those living in that icy environment. A young Nevada woman also used a snowcat to climb an otherwise inaccessible mountain to count its hardy residents. Another enumerator rode an aerial tram to a tungsten mine in California. When the tram broke on the return trip, he had to fight his way down through snow 10 feet deep.

*Cartoonist Steve Canyon dramatizes the plight of another conscientious enumerator, laid up at a critical moment.*

*The Census Takers*

A census taker in the north country had to swim through ice-cold water in April to get to an isolated farmhouse; luckily he was able to borrow a rowboat for the return trip. In Hawaii the water temperature is milder, and census takers often paddle outrigger canoes to island villages. In some isolated areas, aircraft are the only means of getting there and back. Census takers may be transported to islands by Coast Guard helicopter. One in Minnesota reported an exciting flight over lakes and woods, during which he saw moose, wolves, and other wild animals. Among his equipment was a shotgun for protection against the wolves (for which a bounty was paid), and snowshoes in case the plane's engine failed!

## ALL IN A DAY'S WORK

The enumerator often performs services far beyond merely taking the census, like the one who was interviewing a minister when a young couple came in to be married. The interview had to stop while the minister performed the ceremony, with the enumerator serving as a witness to the marriage vows. A housewife had an even more challenging experience—interviewing the residents of a nudist camp. She met with half a dozen unclad men and women in the shade of a large oak tree, while young children cavorted about in their birthday suits. "I tried to look directly at them and see their personalities," she recalled. "It was quite pleasant, so peaceful, so beautiful—you didn't notice the bodies." Her husband couldn't believe it when she told him about it.

Another census taker found a woman unconscious in a small mountain cabin, rushed her to the hospital, and probably saved her from dying of spotted fever. Others have saved small children from burning, adults from asphyxiating in gas-filled rooms, and a couple from rolling into a lake in their car. Not always does this unexpected aid come in time, of course; on some occasions enumerators have come to count the living and had to report new death statistics instead.

A rural census taker arrived at a farmhouse just as a baby was about to be born. Rising to the emergency, the enumerator delivered a baby boy. Later, when she asked the mother what the baby would be named, she was told "Quitten."

161

"You mean *Quentin*, don't you?" she asked.

"Nope," the woman said emphatically. "He's our eighth and last child. That's why we're namin' him Quitten!"

An even more unusual name was chosen for her child by an expectant mother who served as a census taker in 1970. She named her son Fosdic, for the machine that translated her questionnaires into computer tapes.

Census takers report many comical answers to their questions. When one asked the father of a very large family just how many children he had, the man replied, "How many do you need to meet your quota?"

There are often unusual answers to the question, "What is your occupation?" At one home the family business was making caskets, and those who lined them claimed to be "interior decorators." One housewife classified her husband as a piddler: "He just piddles around doing one thing and another." A hippie said his occupation was being a friend to man. In another hippie family, a young man listed himself as "head of the household," the young woman with whom he lived as "friend of the head of the household," and the couple's five-year-old child as "daughter of the friend of the head of the household."

A man classing himself as an inventor offered the census taker his latest invention, a device that would cure any disease in a week. The price: $1 million! Rare occupations included gum taster, golf-ball winder, professional mourner, rug cutter, snake doctor, mouse farmer, subterranean architect, plumber's helper's helper, and artificial limb breaker-inner. There was even a "pickpocket" of the legal variety—one who searched the pockets of clothes brought in for cleaning.

Ages are sometimes determined in strange ways. A census taker working on an Indian reservation had the task of getting the correct ages for 23 children in one family. She hit on the logical idea of arranging them according to height. The mother was then asked to give their ages and did quite well until she stumbled at number 10. At last she remembered, "yes, he came the year of the big snow!" For number 15, she recalled that "this one came the year the salmon run in the river was so light!"

One aged woman interviewed for the 1960 census swore she was born in 1815; an old man remembered George Washington; and a woman claimed to be only 38, even though her son was 33. Enumerators don't find many women aged 30 or men aged 40—Jack Benny was not the only one who was 39 and holding.

The cleanest family yet reported in a census had 4 bedrooms and 6 bathrooms! At another place an enumerator asked if there was running water in the house. "No," said the housewife brightly, "but I'll be glad to go turn the faucet on if you want me to."

Mistaken identity sometimes slows down the business of census taking. One young woman enumerator was greeted at the door of a building by a solicitous older woman. "Don't you worry about a thing, my dear," she said gently. "We just want to help you."

"But I'm with the Census Bureau," the puzzled girl said.

"Oh, my goodness!" the older woman said apologetically. "This is the Home for Unwed Mothers, and I thought. . . ."

A young male census taker knocked on a door and was told to come in and wait a minute. "I'll be right back," the young woman promised and disappeared down the hall. He waited patiently for twenty minutes before she returned, dressed in an evening gown.

"Let's go," she said eagerly, reaching for his arm.

"Go where?" he demanded. "I'm the census taker!"

"Oh, no!" the girl said. "I thought you were my blind date."

As one female census taker entered an apartment, the man inside quickly peeled off his shirt.

"What are you doing?" the enumerator cried, backing toward the door.

"Showing you my incision," was the answer. "Aren't you the visiting nurse?"

In general, enumerators find the people they visit helpful in responding to the census. In Idaho, for example, many residents of outlying areas reversed the normal procedure and came into town to be counted. Their transportation included everything from tractors to horseback to snowshoes. A snowshoer in another state trekked from his remote cabin to the county road so he would be listed. One woman enumerator knocked on a door and heard a feeble voice inside ask her to please climb in the window. An

85-year-old man was lying helpless on the floor. "My census form is in the other room," he said apologetically. "It's all filled out." Before checking it, the enumerator helped the invalid into bed and called a doctor for him.

A frequent bonus is a home-cooked meal. One enumerator had nine dinner invitations while conducting her census work, and several of her hosts and hostesses asked her to come back again and visit when her census work was done. Many respondents welcome the chance to talk, and one emphasized how pleased she was to see the enumerator, her first visitor in more than two years! One census taker claimed the hardest part of the job was not to get people talking but to get them to stop. "One lady took fifteen minutes to tell me about all the proposals she had turned down before she finally told me she was married!" While some people objected to the census, one family proudly attached a family portrait to their questionnaire.

Not all respondents are pleasant and cooperative, of course. A farmer in Texas told the census taker he was too busy plowing to stop and talk to her; she had to conduct the interview by yelling one question each time he drove by. And a Kansan interviewed one of her respondents by shouting questions up at him as he repaired his roof in a strong wind.

One conscientious enumerator called on a householder several times without finding him. On her way home after the last attempt, she was stopped for speeding by a motorcycle policeman—who turned out to be the missing householder! After receiving a ticket, she interviewed him on the spot. On another occasion an escaped convict was thought to be hiding out in an enumeration district. The census taker asked her supervisor what to do if she came across the man. "Just interview him and get his information," was the order.

In 1950, stuntman Digger O'Dell was interviewed for the census atop a flagpole in St. Louis. In 1960 an enumerator had to question him through a small air shaft leading to the "tomb" O'Dell had been buried in as a stunt.

Census experiences register deeply at times, and one enumerator woke her husband in the middle of the night by crying out,

"How many snakes do you have? I have to count the snakes!" Snakes are just one of the many varieties of animals enumerators are exposed to. One had to endure a parakeet sitting on her head and eyeing the census form, meanwhile reciting sonnets from Shakespeare. Another was shaken when, instead of a human, a chattering monkey greeted her at the door. At another house a mother cat proudly brought in her four kittens and placed them at the enumerator's feet. For an encore, she brought in a live mouse.

A woman census taker in a rural area managed to clamber over a fence just ahead of two angry bulls—only to be bitten by a goose on the other side. A donkey harassed another female census taker trying to reach a farm. Later, the same woman was attacked by a turkey until she was saved by the farmer, who came to her aid wielding a broom. On leaving the farm, the enumerator again was attacked by a turkey.

Another woman was alarmed by a sign warning of a fierce dog that bit. Luckily she got into the house with no sign of him. When she asked about it, the lady of the house told her pleasantly, "Oh, he only bites people when they *leave!*" Census training includes a warning to stay out of range of hostile dogs until the owner can call the animal off. One enumerator instead carried doughnuts to bribe the dogs; the treat worked so well she then had trouble getting rid of the animals.

A Hot Springs, Arkansas, enumerator was chased by a duck; a Bluefield, West Virginia, enumerator by a Brahma bull; and a Charlotte, North Carolina, enumerator was treed by a rooster. In Providence, Rhode Island, an enumerator was chased by a goat; a more peaceful goat in Oklahoma merely ate the census taker's stock of completed forms.

Animals are not the only census hazard, of course. One lady census taker went into a shop only to have her nylons disappear from her legs! She went back home and put on another pair, which also vanished as soon as she entered the shop again. It turned out that acid fumes from a faulty storage battery were dissolving the nylon.

An irate housewife chased one census taker down the street with an ax, yelling that her age was "none of the government's damn business!" A milder critic used a fly swatter to chase away a female enumerator, and the woman was later sprayed with a hose as she tried to interview a man washing his car. Another interviewer was hit by a beer can thrown by an angry citizen.

Census taking is similar around the world, and enumerators in other countries have had their share of adventures, too. For example, in Baia, Brazil, a census taker asked a farmer if his daughter was a maiden, not realizing that in that region the word refers to a girl seduced and abandoned, and was thrashed by the farmer for the insult. A much more unfortunate Tanzanian census taker was eaten alive by a crocodile, and in some parts of Africa where some natives fear their children may die if counted, census takers have been killed by angry mobs. There is no record of a census taker in the United States ever having been killed in the line of duty, although one in New Mexico was shot with a revolver by an angry citizen.

It is not just enumerators who are confronted by displeased respondents. After the 1970 census, a woman wrote to Commerce Secretary Maurice H. Stans to say that the census form was "blatant sexism" because a married woman must identify herself as "wife of the head." It wasn't fair, she wrote, because a married man didn't have to check a box for "husband of the head." She considered it insulting to the dignity of female human beings for the census form to refer to a woman as "wife of the head."

On the other hand there was the husband who called his local census office about the question that describes "complete kitchen facilities" as a sink with piped water, a range or cookstove, and a refrigerator. "You mean I didn't have to buy my wife the clothes washer and dryer, the dishwasher, the freezer, the pop-up toaster, the electric can opener, the blender, the beater, and all those other gadgets?" he demanded.

## THE "PERMANENT PART-TIME" WORKERS

The decennial census is taken only once every ten years, and published results take another year or more to reach those who use such information. The need for more up-to-date data is critical in many areas, so the Bureau of the Census conducts continuing surveys, including its Current Population Survey. Each month, always on the nineteenth (except at Christmastime), an army of "permanent part-time" census interviewers take to their territory. Just three weeks later, responses from 66,000 households are in published form for use by government, business, and individuals.

Employment information is vital to the Bureau of Labor Statistics and other planners, inside government and out. The Current Population Survey provides such statistics: not just the number of people out of work, but how many of them are men and how many women, how many are minority workers, how many are teenagers, as well as where they live and what lines of work they are in.

In addition to the Current Population Survey and other continuing surveys, special, one-time efforts are conducted. These include the Survey of Disabled, the Survey of Income and Education, the Survey of Registration and Voting, and the Crime Survey. But it is the Current Population Survey that is most used.

The 10-year census quizzes some 86 million households; the Current Population Survey, only a relative handful. For such a small sampling to be valid it must reflect a specially selected cross-section of America. Key to the sample is the "Primary Sampling Unit," or PSU. There are 1,913 of these in America, one in each of the SMSAs, plus many more as counties or groups of counties. From the 1,913 PSUs the Bureau uses 449 as sample areas to represent the entire nation; it then selects Enumeration Districts, or EDs, from these. Within the EDs, a half dozen or so households are selected as part of the continuing CPS sample. After four months of surveys, a household is omitted for the next eight months and then picked up again for four months. This provides the needed continuity of households, without wearing out the householder's patience and the interviewer's welcome.

There are about a thousand part-time CPS interviewers, many of whom have been on the job for years. Most of them are housewives, but there are also retirees, students, artists, and others. Because CPS people work so much, great care is spent in training them and keeping them trained. In fact, about 15 percent of the budgeted amount for CPS is spent for training and the continuous monitoring of interviewers.

In Mansfield, Ohio, a CPS interviewer visits a thousand homes every fifteen months, with questions on employment, income, nationality, and even what highways are traveled to work and on trips. In all that time and with thousands of questions, only 6 householders have refused to give the information.

A young woman interviewer with the Seattle Regional Office considers the people she has gotten acquainted with worth all the refusals and abuse she gets. Working in San Joaquin County, she became particularly fond of an old couple living on an overgrown 12-acre vineyard. Both dressed in ragtag clothes and wore hats. The woman's hat rested on top of a small bun of hair, while two curly strands dangled on each side of her wrinkled face.

On her first visit, the interviewer was afraid of the place, an unpainted shack at the end of a dirt road. But the couple were friendly from the start, and surprisingly well informed. Both spoke excellent English and discussed current topics intelligently. Eight interviews took place in a year, and in addition to getting answers to her questions the interviewer learned when their well ran dry, making it necessary to borrow water from neighbors. She was pleased that the old man took the trouble to learn and remember her name, and thankful that the Census Bureau made it possible for her to be in touch with such people.

Perhaps not typical of field interviewers is one who works for the Los Angeles Regional Office, and takes dog bites—five of them in one year—and an interview with a naked man in stride. She says her interviews are successful because she is assertive and aggressive, can take care of herself, and likes to see what's happening to the people she works with.

Part of her success stems from an ability to listen to people talk about their problems, likes, and dislikes. She also remains neutral when she asks the questions on her survey. "I'm acting as a machine. When I do the crime surveys, I have to ask people if they've been raped the same way I ask them if they've had a plant stolen." Doors have been slammed in her face, but only a few times has she been turned down completely. Several times she has written letters to people who refused to talk and had them relent and invite her back. The interview with the unclad man came completely by surprise. The census interviewer was holding her book in front of her when he answered the door, and not until she lowered it did she notice the situation. "I just kept on interviewing the man, and that was that."

## THE CENSUS TAKERS

The idea of census takers and other workers being appointed politically has worried many people for more than sixty years, and probably ever since the first census. In 1918, the American Statistical Association drafted a resolution urging that the appointment of supervisors and enumerators be taken out of the hands of politicians. The ASA suggested instead that hiring be done through the Civil Service Commission. A special review committee appointed by the Secretary of Commerce in 1954 called the political hiring of census workers "the legacy of an outmoded past," and again strongly recommended impartial staffing of the census effort.

In spite of continuing complaints, politics still plays a part in census recruiting. For example, Arizona Republicans "referred" census candidates in 1970; in 1980 it was the Democrats because a change in political fortunes elected a Democrat as president. Through the referral system, people are recruited for key supervisory jobs, and also for the many enumerator and clerk jobs. However, other channels are also used, including radio and television, newspaper advertising, and employment-office publicity. All candidates, referrals and others alike, must take tests prepared by the Bureau of the Census to demonstrate that they are capable of doing the work they have applied for. The "political spoils" system, if it can really be called that, actually works quite well in hiring large numbers of people for a short time and at relatively low pay. Tests prepared by the Bureau of the Census also guard against flagrant favoritism. Highly skilled people often agree to help out as a public service.

To be considered for employment as an enumerator for the 1980 census, an applicant had to be a United States citizen, be 18 years old or older, and able to pass the written test demonstrating ability to understand printed instructions and to do simple arithmetic. An

"Enumerator Variance Study" made during the 1950 census proved the value of screening all temporary employees, including district managers, crew leaders, and enumerators. Those who made high scores on the tests were found to leave fewer questions unanswered on the census questionnaires they checked. This correlation between higher test scores was proved again during the 1960 census.

The multiple-choice test includes questions and problems on vocabulary, arithmetic, following directions, reading comprehension, and filling the census questionnaire. A sample question might be: "Mrs. Jones can't remember the year of her birth, but she knows that she was born in the month of April. If it is now May 1980, and Mrs. Jones tells you she is 78, what year was she born?"

Eligibility for a position depends on a score high enough for that position, with crew leaders required to score higher than enumerators. A crew leader may be required to staff his or her own district if sufficient enumerators have not been hired by the time he or she has completed training. Office clerks and enumerators may be hired under the heading of "enumerator-clerk" so that if necessary they may be reassigned without a great deal of administrative paper work. Salaries for census workers in 1970 ranged from $2.15 to $6.40 an hour, depending on the type of work and the location.

## TRAINING

Training for the census-taking effort is done by the "cascade" method, with top personnel training those who will report to them, and so on down to the last enumerator in the field. The training begins in headquarters in Suitland, Maryland, where the regional staff trains its top supervisors, regional technicians, district managers, field supervisors, and office supervisors. These supervisory personnel then train those directly responsible to them. Wherever possible, the person responsible for the performance of a group trains that group. Crew leaders, for example, train their own crews of enumerators.

The basic training tool is the "Verbatim Training Guide," complete for all phases of the job being taught. Questions and expected answers, training exercises, tests and answer keys, and other teaching devices are included. The amount of time to be spent on each portion of the training, the breaks to be taken, and the lunch times are printed in the inside cover of the guide.

As much as possible, training takes place on the site where the actual census work will be done. For example, regional technicians, district managers, and other supervisors are trained in the region where they will work. Clerks are usually trained right at their work stations, crew leaders in the district office, and enumerators in local rent-free sites including post offices, schools, libraries, church halls, and firehouses. The training sessions for crew leaders and enumerators include not only regular enumeration but special assignments, such as "T-night" and "M-night" enumerations. T-night covers transients in hotels, motels, and other places of lodging; M-night covers missions, jails, and other such locations.

## HOW THE CENSUS TAKERS TAKE THE CENSUS

In 1960, the Bureau of the Census counted nearly 180 million Americans. Coincidentally, this effort required the services of a temporary staff of more than 180,000, working out of 399 temporary offices. By 1970 the population had grown to about 205 million, suggesting the need for about 205,000 temporary workers. However, because about 60 percent of the population received mail-out/mail-back census forms, the 1970 census was carried out with a temporary staff of about 185,000, only 3 percent more than in 1960.

The temporary offices are of three basic kinds: conventional Census District Offices, Decentralized Mail Census District Offices, and Centralized Mail Census Offices. The temporary Census District Office at Casper, Wyoming, was one of 181 set up all over the country. The district manager was hired locally, and his top staff consisted of a field supervisor, a supervisory crew leader, and an administrative clerk. An additional twenty-four crew leaders supervised 360 locally hired temporary enumerators whose task it was to enumerate the 385,000 or so inhabitants of Wyoming.

In late January of 1970 the Casper district manager and his top staff reported to the Bureau of the Census Regional Office in Denver. Here they each were given specialized training, along with those from other cities in the Denver region. Training was complete in mid-February, and the leaders were then ready to begin recruiting crew leaders and enumerators. At the same time, the preparation of kits for enumerators was begun, using materials from the Bureau. By mid-March recruiting was nearly complete, and crew leaders had been trained. On the twenty-eighth of March, mailmen delivered advance short-form questionnaires to each Wyoming household, with instructions for the resident to fill it out and have it ready for the enumerator to pick up on April 1, Census Day.

Now it was the enumerator's turn. Canvassing assigned areas, he or she listed and enumerated each housing unit. The enumerator scanned each questionnaire for completeness, asked follow-up questions, and departed. By April 10, some enumerators had completed their assignments and their work was reviewed by the crew leader prior to sending the returns to the District Office in Casper. Some forms required further work or perhaps a return to the original enumerator for completion and/or cleanup. Further necessary work was done and by the middle of May, the Casper District Office had completed its census mission, and was closed.

Flint, Michigan, was the site of one of 167 Decentralized Mail Census District Offices. As in Casper, the district manager was hired locally for this assignment and given the responsibility for three counties with an estimated population of more than 780,000. His staff consisted of an office supervisor, a field supervisor, and two supervisory crew leaders. This field staff was in charge of the 30 crew leaders and 450 enumerators hired temporarily. Training was completed, and in February and March of 1970 recruits worked to update address lists made and checked months earlier. Missing addresses were added to the lists and questionnaires prepared for them. On March 28 the Postal Service delivered the forms.

*This trainee enumerator was supplied with a special Orientation Kit to help her master her special new duties.*

For three or four days, the Flint District Office functioned as a telephone service center to assist respondents who had problems in filling out the census questionnaires. On April 8, enumerator training began. This was different from that of the Casper enumerators, for the Flint personnel would be mostly checking and editing questionnaires in their homes, sometimes using the telephone to resolve problems. Only questionnaires that could not be completed in this way were returned to respondents personally. Some assignments were completed by the end of April, but another month was required before questionnaires were ready for shipment and the Flint office could be closed.

The temporary District Office at Oakland, California, was typical of 45 Centralized Mail Census Offices. Because of the task of covering more than 460,000 respondents in a large city, the district manager and processing supervisor were permanent employees of the Census Bureau. A field supervisor, three supervisory crew leaders, 40 crew leaders, and 450 enumerators were hired locally. An additional 150 or so processing clerks worked in the Oakland office itself.

The mailing of questionnaires and the follow-up work were similar although more difficult than for the Flint office. For example, special care had to be taken to count people who moved between March 1 and May 1. When all questionnaires were finally checked, a preliminary population count was released and the questionnaires were shipped for processing. The Oakland Office was then closed.

## FINDING FOLKS AT HOME

An obvious census-taking problem is, when is the best time to catch people at home? In earlier censuses with very easy questions, the Bureau assumed that anyone fourteen or older could furnish appropriate answers. Now that there are more questions, and of a more complex nature, it is generally necessary to have an adult answer them. Many surveys are also directed at certain age groups: retired persons, women from 30 to 49, men from 45 to 54. To better the census taker's chances of timing a visit successfully, the Bureau added several questions to the monthly Current Population Survey in November, 1971.

Results were published in a working paper titled "Who's Home When." The most obvious finding of the survey was that it was much harder in 1971 to catch people at home than it had been in 1960. From 8 to 9 A.M. for example, there was a 71-percent chance of finding people home in 1960, but there was only a 57-percent chance in 1971. From 5 to 6 P.M. the chances dropped from 78 percent in 1960 to 74 percent in 1971. People in poverty areas were no more accessible than those in nonpoverty areas. Only the retired were available almost all the time, and the study also noted that they generally welcomed a visit and a chance to talk with the interviewer.

## OCCUPATIONAL HAZARDS

An empty house is a census taker's problem, but in some cases, finding people home is a problem too. Enumerators have reported many problems, including "an abundant roach population which interfered with the interview by crawling all over the interviewer and her forms." At times the hazards are much worse, and in extreme cases a questionnaire is turned in with the report, "Will not return—something thrown at me!"

A career Bureau employee followed up on a number of problem addresses and described his experience as follows:

The occupants of the houses with the vacant apartment were a sullen group. The bleary-eyed head of the household of the first-floor apartment had a bottle on the table and glared silently at me while his wife answered the questions. My experiences apparently were prosaic compared to some I learned from discussions with crew leaders and enumerators, e.g., the lady who had been chased out of a house by a threatening occupant. Although this sort of experience is not a regular occurrence by any means, it need happen to an enumerator only once to be unnerving. Situations in which an enumerator is in real danger are probably rare—but cases of suspicion, sullenness, and vituperative hostility in this area are far above our expected norm. It makes the recruitment and reten-

175

tion of good enumerators exceedingly difficult—and those we retain are necessarily those with strong backs and strong stomachs—their intellectual ability being an incidental or accidental asset. The inevitable concomitant of these conditions is under-enumeration— of both persons and housing units. No enumerator in her right mind, even if she is being paid at an hourly rate, will go through some of the traumatic experiences necessary to do a good job of coverage.

Fortunately, such experiences are the exception and not the general rule. However, roaches, thrown objects, and other hazards connected with census taking contribute to the problem of the missed two to three Americans in every hundred. Without the use of coercive tactics, it is doubtful that an appreciable improvement can be made in this small segment of uncooperative members of society.

## SUMMARY

The census taker today is not exposed to the rigors of his pioneer forerunners. Automobiles and other modern vehicles have taken the place of horses and wagons, and the land is more civilized. Nevertheless, there is still some adventure for those who decide to count heads for the American decennial census.

Census taking is a changing process, far different today than it was a few decades ago and bearing only a faint resemblance to the first census 190 years ago. The process now lies on the fringe of whole new technologies, including mail-out, mail-back forms, computer-assisted telephone interviewing, and measurements carried out by high-flying aircraft or even orbiting satellites. The time is passing when a personal visit by the census taker is the key to the whole operation.

For example, Computer-Assisted Telephone Interviewing (CATI) has been tested by the Bureau of the Census at the University of California at Los Angeles. In this form of census interview, the interviewer wears a headset and a mouthpiece wired to a telephone, and sits at a TV screen and computer terminal keyboard. Questions to be asked are displayed on the screen, and answers are fed into the computer by pressing the appropriate keys on the console. The advantages to this method include more accurate data, greater speed, and simplicity for the interviewer, who has the questions to be asked plainly in view on the screen.

Yet each year there are more enumerators and other temporary workers needed in the gigantic task of counting Americans. The human touch is still required, and will probably continue to be for a long time. The task and the experiences of the census taker are changing, with fewer tales of daring adventure and not as many reports of comical responses. But interesting things continue to befall the census taker, whose job will remain challenging and whose stories will be worth telling.

# 10
# The Users of the Census

The products of the Bureau of the Census are like the oxygen in the air. They are consumed so widely that they are accepted as a matter of course and are so often used after analysis and interpretation by one or more intermediaries that the user does not readily recognize their source or their fundamental value as a base for most other statistics.

*Samuel A. Stouffer*

In the very beginning of census taking in the United States, in spite of the example set by the British Board of Trade, the only users of the information gathered were the Congress and the tax collectors. Slowly, however, others have begun to use the increasing amounts of data turned up in counting our people, their possessions, and products. Today the President and his Cabinet, the federal agencies, and the state and local governments could scarcely function without the input of the billions of facts collected and tabulated by the Bureau of the Census.

A Bureau publication titled "Who Uses the Census?" states that a better question would be "Who Doesn't?" Surely the users are many, and more varied than most of us realize. Congress still is a user, and to a much larger extent now than in 1790. Soon after the President delivers the results of the census of population to Congress, a reapportionment of that body is made. A 1929 Congressional Act requires the President to report state populations both by "major fractions" and "equal proportions." This fine distinction

178

in measuring populations prevented the shift of one congressional seat from Michigan to Arkansas in 1940.

Census population figures give us our fair share of Congressmen, but they are used for much more than that. Although only a handful of Americans know it, nearly every service one can think of depends on census information. Consider the following typical examples.

Congress allocates adult-education funds on the basis of the number of people in a state who are more than 18 years of age with less than 5 years of schooling. And the number of children from ages 5 to 17 in poor families determines the amount of money going to counties through the Elementary and Secondary School Act. Other funding under this act depends on the number of non-English-speaking children in families, information that can come only from the census. Lunch programs, vocational education, vocational rehabilitation, building planning, and the hiring of teachers depends on population in certain age brackets. Child Welfare, the Crippled Children's Services, and Public Health Services also depend on population and other census information.

The Federal Aviation Agency uses population data to implement the Federal Airport Act. Department of Agriculture Extension Services depend on counts of the rural population, equipment, and crops. Revenue sharing for thousands of local governments fluctuates with the census. Census information is also necessary for administering the Economic Opportunity Act, Manpower Development and Training, Higher Education Facilities, Federal Aid to Highways, Appalachian Regional Development, and hundreds of other acts. The states, too, allocate funds on the basis of census population and other figures. Hospitals, libraries, prisons, fire departments, courts, foster homes, pensions, the Civil Service, veterans' aid, parks, timber reserves, livestock shows, weed and pest control, sewage plants, flood control, and snow removal are some of the items administered.

Arizona law requires that there must be 500 people in a town for it to incorporate, and census population data is needed to establish this count. Florida won't permit two shifts of firemen until a town has 15,000 or more residents. In Idaho, cities with more than 5,000

179

must maintain an employment office, whereas those smaller need not. Massachusetts gives funds for each child between 7 and 16 years of age in towns smaller than 5,000. In Oregon, the state supervises traffic signs and signals in cities of less than 50,000; those larger do it for themselves. The Kansas Legislature in a single session passed more than 60 laws based on census population figures. Tennessee real estate agents pay licenses and bonding fees proportional to the population of the county they do business in. In Ohio, city recreation workers documented a correlation between juvenile delinquency and insufficient recreational areas, using census information on population, housing, and income. The study led to the building of more recreational facilities.

Branch libraries and bookmobile services are planned with information on population, age, sex, and income. Even the titles offered and the hours of business depend on the census. Community-action projects are good examples of the use of census data; indeed, most will not get far if such data are not used. Examples are relocation projects, often seen as threats to communities. Adult-education programs, day-care centers, playgrounds, voter registration, and housing improvement are others. All are based on population, housing, age, sex, income, and other census information.

For a long time, Indians were not even counted in censuses. Today most tribes are enthusiastic users of census information. One tribe, wanting to get into the tourism business, used census data on population, income, and other characteristics to launch an advertising campaign for its big-game hunting preserve. Civil-rights organizations, minorities, and the Labor Department all must have figures on income, employment, sex, race, and other characteristics. The White House needs to know about foreign trade and the balance of payments to plan its policy properly, both domestic and foreign.

From time to time special censuses play an important part in solving particular problems. Following the riots in the Los Angeles area, a Watts Survey was conducted by the Census Bureau in an attempt to learn more about unemployment, housing, and income. Other special surveys in the 1960's covered senior citizens and disabled adults. More recently there have been surveys of the results of civil-rights legislation in voting, and those covering crime and its effects. The Manpower Administration and the Social Security Administration have requested special Census Bureau surveys. For the Department of Transportation, the Bureau of the Census has conducted surveys, including "Economic and Social Effects of Traffic Accidents." The Department of Defense in 1964 requested a "Survey of Draft-Age Men."

Columbia University scientists have found that the rate at which people are hospitalized can be predicted from census information about their ethnic composition. Studied were Puerto Ricans, blacks, Jews, Italians, and Irish. The findings included the fact that male mental-hospital admissions for the Brooklyn-Bronx sector were 61 per 1,000, compared with only 38 per 1,000 in the Queens-Staten Island sector. Strangely, the rates for women were 42 per 1,000 in both areas. The study also suggested that lower incomes were a contributing factor in mental illness, with incomes in Queens–Staten Island averaging $11,595 against $8,659 in Brooklyn-Bronx. Data for this work came from the 1970 census.

## DATA-USER SERVICES

The Data User Services Division (DUSD) is an important part of the Census Bureau; its chief considers himself the "marketing manager for a plant producing statistics." Although the Bureau has long worked with users of its information, a formal Data User Services came into being only recently. A Data Access and Use Laboratory was created to help with the 1970 Census, and a Census Use Study was carried out in New Haven, Connecticut to develop applications for some of the Bureau's new "products." Both the Data Access and Use Laboratory and the Census Use Study were later incorporated into what is now the Data User Services Division.

Taking DUSD to the people who needed it, the Bureau's Center for Census Use Studies established the Unified Statistical Evaluation Study, or USES, in Indianapolis. During 1973 the USES office answered 621 research questions from a variety of users in the state. These included government officials (who asked the most questions) market researchers conducting studies for businesses, civic groups, churches, and charitable organizations, educators and students, and the Indiana public in general.

The Mayor's office needed to know how people in Indianapolis

181

got to work. USES quickly reported that 222,337 Indianapolites drove alone, 44,405 rode with others, and that more than 1,000 went by taxi. There were also 59 reported traveling by subway, a statistic that raised eyebrows because Indianapolis has no subway! The computer found that the largest group classed as subway riders lived across from a cemetery, and it was decided that someone was having fun with the survey.

Another question had to do with nutrition centers for the aged. Money was available for just 20 centers, and Indianapolis wanted to know where to put them for the most benefit. USES provided locations that would serve the greatest number of elderly; the cost for the service was only $2.28, and it took only 4 minutes. A similar task for locating adult education centers cost $3.08. The Mayor also called on the Census Bureau for help in car pooling. In 1973 and 1974 he was one of the many who did.

## CARPOL TO THE RESCUE

When the gasoline crunch hit in 1973, the Bureau of the Census responded immediately to President Nixon's urgent request for increased car pooling. Nixon spoke on TV on November 7; on December 11 the Bureau announced its new CARPOL computer programs for any local or municipal government or private employer. The cost? Just $70 for the CARPOL computer tape and instructions for using it. Fieldtested in the Los Angeles area prior to the energy crisis, CARPOL was adopted immediately by many areas needing to increase car pooling. The program made use of the extensive Geographic Base Files/Dual Independent Map Encoded (GBF/DIME) system created by the Bureau for a variety of uses in metropolitan areas.

Computers can do a lot more than just count. They can do mapping as well, and one of the most useful programs the Census Bureau has developed is GBF/DIME. The system has two basic parts: standard geographic elements, such as street name and address, block number, and census tract; plus *local* elements such as police beat, school district (or sales district), political precinct, and so on.

When a mayor or councilman needs population or financial data for planning next year's budget, they most likely get it from the Census Bureau. When the local Community Center needs facts, figures, and maps for a new service for old folks or young folks, chances are they get them because you and your neighbors responded to the last census questionnaire.

From pilot operations a few years ago in Kansas City, Atlanta, and Los Angeles, the Bureau created a strong regional service organization with Data User Services officers in each of the twelve Census regions. DUSD conducted 20 Data Users' Education and Training activities during 1977 and increased that number to 28 in 1978. Sessions were held in Washington, D.C.; Oklahoma City; Ann Arbor, Michigan; Chicago; Minneapolis; Kansas City; Detroit; Boston; Seattle; and Los Angeles.

The Census Bureau collects, processes, and distributes a wide range of data used by businessmen, industrialists, marketers, and planners. These cover the two broad areas of demographics (people) and economics. The 10-year census of population and housing is a gold mine for businessmen and manufacturers, including those planning new ventures or facilities. Information on population, employment, job skills, race, and economic standing aid greatly in marketing. Typical questions answered by DUSD include: What is the ethnic makeup of an area? Would it pay a business to post billboards with its advertising message in Spanish? Is an area populated by the young, old, or a broad range of ages?

## A PAT ON THE BACK FROM THE POLLSTERS

Just before the 1970 census, the Bureau received strong support from Arthur C. Nielsen, Jr., president of the marketing research firm whose "Nielsen ratings" are life or death to TV programs. Nielsen pointed out that although there were only 29 American companies with marketing research departments in 1932, the number had grown to 1235 by 1969. All these organizations, he said, constantly relied on census data. Responses indicated that many marketers had used census data so long it was "like breathing the air around them." Applications included:

183

Allocation of sales effort
Allocation of advertising and promotion
Determination of sales potential by area
Selection of areas for special new products
Forecasting long-term sales trends
Determining locations for facilities
Setting up market surveys
Selecting desirable labor markets

Pointing out the blinders many Bureau critics wear, Nielsen quoted a Congressman who saw no need to fund census statistics on births and deaths, "because my insurance company already publishes such figures," and a Cabinet member who questioned the Census of Business, since "I can get all the business information I need from the manager of the local Sears store." The truth of the matter is that there is no way to estimate the dollar value of the census—except by discontinuing it and then evaluating the chaos that would result in the marketplace.

Talking specifically about what census material his firm used, Nielsen cited the 10-year census information for age, sex, education, income and other details. The "Current Population Survey" and "Marital Status and Living Arrangement" were used to update that basic data. The Nielsen firm then put the results into its own computers to arrive at detailed population profiles from which it randomly chose households for its TV-audience sampling. The cost of the census data to Nielsen was only about $30 a year.

## THE REGIONAL PROGRAM

Government agencies are logical users of census data, but it was surprising to learn of the reverse impact of such data on business. One gets an idea of the scope of this field in talking with a Data User Services officer like Bud Steinfeld in the Los Angeles Regional Office. Just unwinding from one users' seminar, Steinfeld was already preparing for the next, a joint seminar with the Small Business Administration for women in business.

"*Pre*-business workshops," sessions to help those who have just gone into business or are considering it, are also high on the list of user priorities. Steinfeld described a typical attendee, a middle-aged woman who wanted to set up a beauty parlor in a small Los Angeles community. Using techniques including ADMATCH, or Address Matching, he helped the woman pinpoint potential customers in the area she had picked. With UNIMATCH, he expanded the information to include financial status and other helpful indicators. Finishing the analysis with a sampling technique called a "Scattergram," he had most of the would-be beauty shop operator's research done. Coupling population information with that from business censuses of the area, she could conclude with confidence not only that the area would support her shop, but also how much money she and her operators could expect to make.

Another recent client of the Los Angeles DUSD was an equipment manufacturer interested in reaching pilots of light aircraft. The Bureau helped with data on population, income, and so on, then suggested supplementing this with other available information, including voter-registration lists and pilots' organizations. The result was a carefully tailored list of consumers likely to be interested in the manufacturer's product.

Bureau seminars are held for groups including savings-and-loan officials, government planners, educators, PTA groups, and minority organizations. A banker at a savings-and-loan meeting asked why a Census Bureau official was there. "Aren't you interested in *people?*" the Census man countered. "I see your point!" the banker said. "Why haven't you been here *before?*" As an example of its effectiveness, DUSD greatly increased one financial institution's business—in an area the bank had served for many years. The secret was the many geographical coding techniques the Bureau had worked out over the years, and which the bank did not know about.

Another request for Bureau help involved finding out how many residents had come to Los Angeles from Southern states; a prospective restaurant specializing in Southern cooking needed this information before it ordered too many ham hocks and beans. A somewhat different set of data was required by a new racketball court eager to learn where all the jocks lived.

185

The Los Angeles office answers a variety of questions, some not as weighty as others. For example, a producer of the Dinah Shore Show had planned a segment involving Lucille Ball. A comedy bit hinged on the month when Lucille's last child had been born, and the producer wanted to know in which month *most* babies arrive.

"September," Steinfeld responded off the top of his head. "There is an old wives' tale that it has some connection with New Year's resolutions."

Most data-user questions take longer, as this sampling suggests:

A *national supermarket chain* had a vacant lot in what seemed a poor risk industrial area. However, census data on population and housing, plus retail-food-sales surveys, suggested strongly that the site could be a good one. It was, and sales were very close to those predicted in the research analysis.

A *manufacturer of home permanents* forecasts his 5-year production schedules on the basis of the number of girls becoming sixteen each of those years. Census information also makes it possible to distribute accurate quantities in each area he serves.

An *oil company* sought help in locating a refinery in an area of cheap land, with no large population nearby, and close to a market for byproduct fertilizer. The Census Bureau helped find a bargain tract close to a small town—whose tobacco growers bought the fertilizer.

A *life insurance company* in New England uses census statistics on population and the value of owner-occupied homes to plan ahead for sufficient capital for future mortgage loans.

A *firm renting formal wear* in two cities used population data including age, sex, education, and income to site an additional hundred stores in just two years.

A *maker of power tools* for home craftsmen checked census statistics on family income and number of rooms per household. His advertising was then increased in wealthier areas with larger houses and sales increased nearly 100 percent.

A *radio station* on the Gulf Coast documented a sizable increase in population from census figures to justify an increase in its advertising rates.

A *manufacturer of school buses* uses census population statistics and projections for the years ahead to help school officials plan the number of buses they will need in the future.

A *construction firm* bidding on a municipal waste disposal plant used census population projections to select a site 20 miles from town to avoid crowding from a rapidly expanding population.

A *hospitalization insurance firm* used population projections to study future population by age group, and thus measured the potential market for its policies.

*Urban Transportation Systems Associates* of Newton, Massachusetts, uses the Census Bureau's GBF/DIME files and the UNIMATCH program for on-board bus surveys (trip purpose, car ownership, occupation, etc.) in the Boston area. The firm also designed a vehicle-miles-traveled estimating procedure and an accident-locating and reporting system using UNIMATCH in Rhode Island.

*Magazine publishers* use census data to find areas where residents have a high level of education, and then advertise heavily in these area. The report "Book Industry Trends—1978" used census data to point out the massive changes in population, income, and book buying that argue for different methods of bookselling. The authors used census data and tables including "Population by Geographic Area," "Bookstores by Geographic Area," and "Book Sales by Geographic Area." Their conclusions: bookselling is a remarkable growth industry, but most booksellers continue to "drift with traditional industry averages of performance." The evidence clearly showed that census data is a strong tool for improvement.

## COMMERCIAL DATA SERVICES

There is a limit to how much census information can be published by the Bureau, and often this is insufficient for special user needs. In such cases it is necessary to go back to "summary tapes" produced by census computers and extract the needed data. A decennial census produces about 2000 reels of tape, at $80 a reel, and only rarely would it pay a user to buy them all. It is generally cheaper to use a commercial data service. In addition to its own data-processing centers, the Census Bureau recognizes more than a hundred private, governmental, and academic organizations as "Summary Tape Processing Centers." A listing of these centers shows them in forty-five states, with ten in California alone.

When I decided to look into this area of census-data use, I didn't have to look far. A good friend and former neighbor had established such a service in Phoenix. One of a dozen such services in the state, Data Dimensions, Ltd., is affiliated with a national organization called Continental Financial Corporation. Data Dimensions has many clients, and a variety of services. A recent mailing of brochures went to 8,500 businesses across the country.

Among current clients are a national appliance distributor interested in learning water hardness statistics throughout the nation for use in a sales campaign for an ice maker. A franchise drug firm requested information on competition in the area, plus age information for residents of various areas. A well-known national auto-servicing firm had commissioned a study leading to better identification of potential customers. A real-estate firm wanted income, age, and education statistics for the area it served. A large land developer, new to the state, had similar questions.

A national fast-food chain required traffic data plus a profile of an "ideal user" of its services. A small local insurance agency was searching for accurate information on areas with the most young married couples. It also required data on age, income, and number of cars in each household. Banks and savings-and-loan associations need special reports on mortgage holders to comply with the recent "Regulation C" federal requirements.

Hospitals are Data Dimension clients, as are fundraisers who want to use the "rifle" rather than the "shotgun" approach in mail, phone, and personal solicitations. Community action groups like Phoenix's Valley Forward require accurate population and economic data to plan ongoing campaigns for civic improvement.

As we discussed his work, my friend explained how effective the "information map" approach is. Instead of stacks of hard-to-interpret raw statistics, clients receive a color-coded map that shows them at a glance where they are selling or not selling; where high income or low income households are located; or where rentals predominate over private houses.

"We've only scratched the surface of possible uses of organized data," Data Dimension says. "Before long there will hardly be a business that can survive without taking this approach." The Census Bureau facilitates such efforts as it works toward gathering more data, and more accurate data, not only in traditional areas but in new ones as well.

## IMPROVING DATA-USER SERVICES

Nobody wins them all, and users are sometimes unhappy with census information. In 1960 the Bureau classified housing units as "sound," "deteriorating," or "dilapidated." Householders had such a difficult time deciding what condition their homes were in that their responses were of little value to anyone. The 1970 classification was changed and was based on plumbing, heating, value, and rent.

Some years ago a task force headed by Carl Kaysen, Director of Princeton's Institute for Advanced Study, criticized the Census Bureau for more serious faults. The strongest complaint was the time lag between the receipt of information and its availability to users in an effective form. A second problem was the lack of "micro-information," or minute detail in census data. The Kaysen report said that the Bureau tended to publish totals and averages rather than specific facts.

While looking at a set of census maps for Arizona's Maricopa County where I lived, I saw how race information is suppressed in detailed block maps. The overriding concern of the Bureau is the preservation of confidentiality; if a sample is small enough for individuals to be identified, the information is suppressed.

The Kaysen Report admitted that confidentiality made it difficult to preserve the detail they sought, but stated that present technology made it possible to accomplish both goals. A particular complaint was the "rather gross geographical breakdown" of census data. The Bureau responded by refining geographical data, and also by placing less emphasis on the publication of formal documents and more on the data itself and on ways of making it available in the most useful form. As an example, the Bureau has worked hard to make its computer tapes—once compatible with only certain com-

189

puters—more versatile and therefore more useful. These tapes contain far more of the "micro-information" the Kaysen Report favored.

Other problems of the Bureau of the Census come from its dedication to the principle of calling the shots the way it sees them. In reporting statistics in 1974, for example, the census Bureau cited 4 times as much crime as did the FBI. The Bureau has also staged a running battle with the Agency for International Development on the economic status of foreign nations that are assisted byAID. Indeed, AID has been charged with suppressing information that did not reflect to its credit.

A former employee blamed the Census Bureau for the business recession of 1974, charging that the Bureau held back information far too long and thus weakened the confidence of businessmen. At least such charges are not about what the Bureau is doing—or not doing—but the complaint is that it is not doing what it does fast enough. For example, during a 1974 hearing conducted in Miami by the House Committee on the Census and Statistics, Congressman William Lehman of Florida complained:

> It seems that everyone else knows where the people are: the public school system knows, the utilities, the Florida Power and Light Company and the telephone company, and certainly the immediate people know where the people are. I think it's derelict of the Census Bureau to be always so far behind in their data, as many of the other public or semipublic sources seem to have the data available and ready at hand.

Such charges are frequent, sometimes backed with proof that millions of dollars have been lost in revenues because of late data. Instead of trying to excuse itself, the Census Bureau is trying to speed up its processes.

## IMPROVING THE CENSUS PRODUCT

A paper prepared for the Census Advisory Committee of the American Marketing Association in May of 1978 indicated the

Bureau's own dissatisfaction with its performance. The introduction pointed out that although the Census Bureau is a public agency without a sales/profit motive, it is charged with the responsibility of collecting and publishing statistics of value to the Congress, federal agencies, state and local governments, private enterprise, academic organizations, nonprofit research, community-service organizations, trade associations, and neighborhood groups.

More must be done than simply publishing 4,000 documents a year, the Bureau admits, pointing out that after 190 years of census taking, potential users of the statistics gathered still outnumbered actual users. Consequently, the Bureau is continuously stepping up its marketing program to reach "customers." That program consists of activities similar to those used by the private sector: marketing research, promotion, distribution, education, and support. The following are examples of those activities.

*Marketing Research*: This includes such things as the 73 public hearings conducted around the country to help plan the 1980 census, the responses from more than 10,000 subscribers to *1980 Census Update*, a number of user surveys, and input from nine census advisory committees.

*Promotion*: The Bureau is limited by the fact that paid advertising cannot be used in "promoting" its products. However, its exhibits at 65 trade and professional conventions in 1978 made it possible to talk with and provide material to more than 100,000 current or potential census-data users. Announcements and press releases are sent to thousands of relevant outlets.

*Distribution*: This is handled through the U.S. Government Printing Office, more than 1,000 Federal Depository Libraries around the country, and more than 100 Census Bureau Depository Libraries. Most other major public and academic libraries stock copies of Census reports, as do many city-planning departments, chambers of commerce, and regional planning and economic development organizations. Other outlets include the more than 100 public and private Summary Tape Distribution Centers. There is also a new State Data Center Program being set up.

*Education and Training*: The Bureau offers a variety of conferences, workshops, seminars, and courses. Survey courses of benefit

191

to state and local government personnel and librarians are offered several times a year. Another educational activity is the College Curriculum Support Project. Under its guidance, material is put into college-level courses in sociology, geography, business, urban planning, library science, and other disciplines to introduce students to census "products." More than 1,000 instructors use these materials.

*Product Support*: To provide close support directly from the 200 specialists available through Data User Services, the Bureau distributed more than 150,000 copies of its Telephone Contact List to users and potential users. Proof of the effectiveness of this step was the initial cry from some Bureau personnel to "get my name off that list—I can't get any work done for the phone ringing!" However, they soon appreciated the fact that this response to users was important work.

## STATE DATA CENTER PROGRAM

As part of the campaign to get more information to users, on September 12, 1978, Director Manuel Plotkin announced the establishment of the Census Bureau's State Data Center Program, calling it one of the most significant advances in improving the public's ability to acquire and use census data.

"For the first time," Plotkin said, "we will have formally organized Federal-State cooperatives expanding and speeding the availability of census information for users in state and local governments, universities, businesses, trade associations, and minority organizations."

The program began with Alabama, Arizona, Louisiana, and North Carolina as pilot states. Most others were expected to join the program prior to the 1980 census. The Census Bureau will provide participating states with material resources such as statistical reports and computer tapes, reference reports, and maps. Information will cover all census statistical programs, including population and housing, manufacturing, agriculture, distributive trades, and service industries. The Bureau will also provide the training and technical assistance for State Data Center staffs, plus consultation on special problems. State Data Centers will provide user services such as tape processing, library facilities, inquiry handling, training, consultation, and general assistance in using census data. States will pay for space, personnel, and administration.

"The Bureau's main interest is to provide for improved dissemination of census products," Plotkin said. "Additionally, a major advantage to the Bureau will be the regular feedback we get on the value of the data we are providing and on the forms and packaging of the data. This information will help us improve our statistical programs and be more responsive to user needs. We will benefit not only in the decennial censuses, but in the agricultural and economic censuses taken every five years, and in population and housing surveys."

The State Data Center Program has been designed to use existing facilities and resources to the fullest extent to avoid any unnecessary governmental expansion either in Washington or in member states. Though improving user services, the program will not create any additional reporting burden on the public.

## SUMMARY

In the beginning, the census was looked upon by nearly everyone (even the underpaid census takers!) as a necessary evil. Answering a lot of nosy questions took time and, worst of all, it cost taxpayers money for a lot of useless paperwork that probably would end up in the trash heap. But it didn't. Most of it is still available, and is actually returning a profit for the expense the nation was put to in collecting it.

Who uses the census? The President does, and so does his Cabinet. The Congress does, too. And so do some 39,000 government entities across the land. Business is a user too, and it is here that the greatest increases in such use are taking place. Advertisers use the census information, and that means that just about all businesses do. There is even a booming new business that has grown up just to handle census information. And whether you are aware of it or not, you are using the census yourself in some way.

Who uses the census? Just about everybody, that's all!

# 11
# The 1980 Census

In the rapidly developing science and practice of statistical sampling, there can be little doubt that American universities and government institutions—notably the United State Bureau of the Census—lead the world.
                                                                *Donald R. Belcher*

The 1980 census is our first billion-dollar census. This is more than $4 for every man, woman, and child in the United States, but it is a bargain for the amount of information produced. It is interesting, nevertheless, to compare the price tag of the twentieth census with the first one in 1790. That initial effort cost only about $44,000, about *a penny* per head counted.

There is another great difference between the two censuses. That first census and many that followed were done from scratch, with an organization hurriedly put together. Almost as soon as the counting was finished, the temporary census staff vanished, leaving an "out-for-the-decade" sign on the door for anyone who might come seeking information. In contrast, the 1980 census has the benefit of a large, well-trained standing organization—one that has not been on vacation between 1970 and 1980, but has been spending much of its time in preparation for this greatest of all censuses.

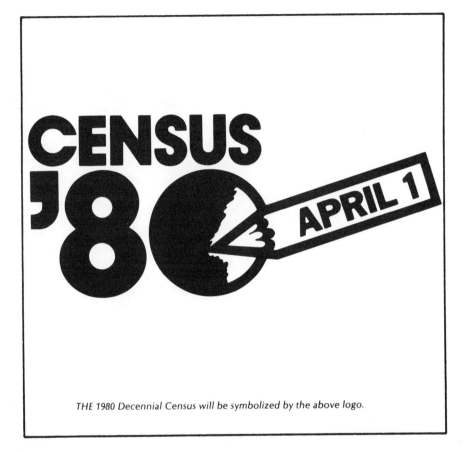

*Despite its many batteries of powerful new machines, the Bureau chose the lowly pencil to symbolize its 1980 campaign.*

Not that this census hasn't had its problems. Early in 1979 there were rumblings in the Bureau that suggested all was not well. With little more than a year to go before the taking of the 1980 Census, rumors flew that director Manuel Plotkin, appointed just two years earlier by President Carter, was in trouble with the Administration and with his bosses in the Department of Commerce. Praised by his workers as hardworking, honest, and professionally competent, Plotkin was nevertheless faulted as being politically naive, incapable of coping with a hostile outer world, and increasingly losing the confidence of his staff.

Bringing matters to a head was a "60 Minutes" television interview of Plotkin that showed him in a poor light, and the early retirement of key Bureau officials, including Deputy Director Robert Hagan, and veteran Bureau experts David Kaplan, Harold Nissleson, and James Turbitt. Perhaps the last straw was the fact that Plotkin had been named as defendant in a suit brought against the Bureau by Sears, Plotkin's former employer.

In the face of all of this, Plotkin tendered his resignation. President Carter then appointed former Director of the Census Vincent P. Barabba to replace Plotkin.

Barabba, a former information specialist in the Air Force, completed degrees in marketing and business administration. He worked for Nelson Rockefeller in the latter's primary fight against Barry Goldwater, and soon thereafter formed a research firm called Datamatics, which used census information in its services. A Republican, Barabba conducted polls for candidates including Richard Nixon. When Nixon entered the White House in 1973, he put Barabba in the job of Director of the Census.

The appointment was political, but Barabba soon proved that he was equal to the task. Besides his political savvy and ingratiating manner, he soon demonstrated an understanding of the new job and an ability to win over his staff and ably fight their battles with Commerce and the administration and Congress.

## LAUNCHING DAY

On Tuesday, April 1, 1980, the twentieth decennial census began. It included 3,100 counties; 20,000 incorporated villages, towns, and cities; 35,000 county subdivisions; 45,000 census tracts; 275,000 enumeration districts; and 2,500,000 city blocks. When it is complete, some 39,000 government entities will use the resulting data to receive their share of $50 billion in revenue funds.

For the first time, census questionnaires were mailed to practically every household in the United States. About 90 percent were asked to mail back their completed questionnaires; the others were asked to hold them for census takers to pick up. One household in six was selected at random to receive the long-form questionnaire; all others received the short form. A massive public information campaign, aided by the National Advertising Council, encouraged the return of mail questionnaires promptly. The census will be more useful as more participate, and each additional 1 percent mail response will also save taxpayers an estimated $2 million in enumeration costs.

Census officials have estimated the total count of Americans in the 1980 census to be about 222 million, only a 9-percent increase from the 1970 population, and one of the smallest increases in history. The fastest-growing state is probably Alaska, with a 35-percent increase. Next comes Nevada, at 30 percent; Arizona, 29 percent; and Florida, 25 percent. The fastest-growing region is that including the mountain states, with a 21 percent overall increase. California again tops the states in population, with more than 22 million. New York remains in second place, but Texas replaces Pennsylvania as third largest.

In its prime function as reapportioner of the Congress, the 1980 census will probably result in Florida's gaining an additional 4 seats and New York's losing 4. Texas will most likely gain 2 seats whereas Illinois, Ohio, and Pennsylvania will each lose 2. Arizona, California, Oregon, Tennessee, Utah, Maryland (home of Census Bureau headquarters), and Colorado will each gain a seat; Michigan, South Dakota, and Missouri will each lose one. As an example of how close the balance can be in reapportionment, the 435th seat in 1970 was decided by a population difference of less than 300.

Although households have increased to about 86 million, there are proportionately fewer families and more nonfamily households. In 1980, an estimated 5.5 million women over 65 live alone but men in this category total less than 1.5 million. Unmarried couples living together have tripled from the 1970 count of 500,000 to a total of 1.5 million.

Women have closed the gap with men on college completion, and blacks have made further significant education gains compared with whites. Women also have jumped from 42 percent of the labor force in 1970 to perhaps slightly more than 50 percent in 1980.

Overall, there are more aged nonworkers to be supported by the job holders. Median family real income increased 34 percent between 1960 and 1970, but that happy trend has been stopped in its tracks. In 1980 the increase is only about 4 percent above the 1970 figures.

About 26 million black people are being counted, an increase of 3.5 million since 1970. This represents abut 12 percent of the total population. The Spanish-origin population totals about 13 million, most of them Mexican-Americans. The 1980 census also provides information on Vietnamese and Koreans as they find a place in America's still-simmering melting pot.

## CAMPAIGN 1980

A massive effort is required to get the census job done. Late in 1979, 410 large trucks loaded with census supplies headed out across the nation from a huge warehouse in Jeffersonville, Indiana. This was the opening field movement in a prodigious logistical operation leading up to the twentieth decennial census on April 1, 1980. Each truck was headed for one of 410 temporary district offices covering the nation. From those field offices an army of 280,000 was hired from 1,300,000 applicants and sent into action.

Some of those trucks ended their cross-country journey in Arizona, where they unloaded supplies for the state's 1750-worker task force. Arizona was allocated about $300,000 for the 1970 census effort; the 1980 cost was about $1.5 million. In 1975, the city of Phoenix conducted its own special census because earlier Bureau figures did not reach expected population totals. (Phoenix spent the money in vain; its census turned up no more inhabitants than had the official Bureau effort.) Besides Phoenix, another 406 governmental units in Arizona are eagerly watching the 1980 census because of its importance in revenue sharing.

In 1970, a census supervisor in Arizona casually told the driver of a census supply truck to "just set the things in the carport." The trucker said he didn't think the supervisor understood the situation; when she saw the truck and its huge load she agreed.

A total of 6.1 million pounds of questionnaires was transported to district offices in 1970, and these were only a small portion of the total of 170 different supply items. Also included were 47 manuals and handbooks totaling nearly 4,000 pages, and an additional 60 training guides containing another 10,000 pages. About 107 million of these were printed and trucked around the country.

Even in today's computerized, electronic world, people still make marks on paper. There were 1.15 million black lead pencils, 500,000 colored pencils, and 305,000 pencil sharpeners. Paper cartons totaled 1.8 million, and there were 270,000 large enumerator ID cards and 180,000 plastic enumerator portfolios. For carrying questionnaires in quantity, 200,000 heavy-duty shopping bags were provided.

The Census Bureau long ago learned the virtues of cardboard furniture, so the trucks hauled 250,000 cardboard tables for work stations and another 1,700 for typing tables. Among the many other items were thousands of large trays and wheeled dollies. Obtained locally were 393 printing calculators, 1900 adding machines, and 786 typewriters. When all the smoke cleared away after the census, 11 of the calculators, 54 adding machines, and 11 typewriters were missing. There was no problem with the cardboard furniture, since it is customarily given away to local churches, clubs, or charitable groups.

Big as 1970 was, 1980 made it seem a modest effort. David Kaplan, Assistant Director for Demographic Censuses, headed up the census of population and housing, as he has done in the past. He calls the gigantic effort "our billion-dollar baby," but hastens to remind us that the importance of the census goes far beyond just spending some heavy money. The most important thing, for $1 billion or whatever sum is invested, is what comes out of the census. No longer is mere statistical measurement enough; the census must make an accounting that is far more than just raw material for another *World Almanac*.

In Kaplan's words, the census has become an "action instrument" largely determining how the nation's social, economic, and political pie is cut up. The bureau's "shadowy existence in a world of passionate anonymity" is gone, and the news media and the public are now beating a path to Suitland Headquarters with requests, and even demands. This relationship between census takers and users, is what the census is all about, of course.

Since the 1970 census cost only about $1 per capita, the 1980 effort represents roughly a $3 increase in ten years. Kaplan explains the increase as follows: $1, or about one third of the jump, was added by inflation. The next 75 cents was added to finance direct efforts to get better coverage in this census. Another 50 cents was necessary to fund improvements in field administration, an indirect expense toward a better census count. New data requirements increased costs 25 cents; enhanced geographic and processing operations accounted for another 25 cents. The last 25 cents had to be added because average household size has decreased appreciably; it costs more to count 6 people living in 3 different households than the same 6 when they reside in only 2 households.

## PREPARATION

Because we are aware of it only then, we tend to think of the census as a one-year operation every decade. In fact, the decennial census of population and housing is a continuous 10-year operation, occupying many Bureau personnel all the time, and a vast number during the actual year of the census. The only reason work on the 1980 census didn't begin in 1971 was because work continued on the 1970 effort until the end of its "census period" in April, 1973. The 1980 census will be wrapped up only on April 1, 1983—if all goes well!

Behind the first thrusts of the 1980 field operation are many years of the planning and careful preparation so familiar to Bureau officials who have conducted a series of decennial censuses. For example, in August of 1973, David Kaplan flew to Vienna to present a paper titled "Some Current Thoughts on the 1980 Census." Soon afterward, the Census Bureau began hosting conferences at which governmental agencies, businesses, community action groups, and ethnic minorities were asked to help frame questions and shape the statistical details for the next census.

# CENSUS BY THE PEOPLE

In the first several censuses, the American public had no voice at all in the process. Theirs was but to respond to questions framed for them, or pay a penalty. Slowly that one-sided arrangement has been turned around, and now the Bureau spends much of its time in diligently, tactfully, and patiently polling the many segments of America's population for proper questions and palatable procedures appropriate for conducting a census rather than an inquisition. During 1974 and 1975, 73 local public meetings and 16 state agency meetings were held to provide input from users of census data. Feedback from these sessions resulted in a number of changes in the questionnaires.

Typical of these meetings was the one on "Planning for the 1980 Census of Population and Housing," held in May of 1975 in Phoenix, Arizona. Sponsored by the Arizona chapter of the American Statistical Association, it included state and federal agencies as well as businesses. The purpose of the meeting was to suggest improvements in Census Bureau procedures and in the use of census information in the State of Arizona. Among suggestions from sponsors and individual citizens were the following:

The Bureau of the Census, in concert with NASA, the Department of the Interior, and the Arizona Resources Information System should conduct aircraft overflights in specified areas of Arizona concurrently with the decennial census, or as soon thereafter as practical.

The Bureau should return to its public hearing sites to report its strategies for improving accuracy in counting ethnic and bilingual groups. This should take place before final decisions on the questionnaire and its methodology and implementation.

The Bureau should issue a clear and specific public assurance that information regarding citizenship and year of immigration will remain anonymous and not be used to identify or locate individuals of questionable legal status.

Census staffing should be divorced from political patronage.

In all areas where there are known bilingual groups with language barriers, census takers should be bilingual. It may also be helpful to employ an Indian from the surveyed community as a canvasser to ensure that all Indians are surveyed.

Arizona Indian reservations should be excluded from the mail-out/ mail-back census forms.

The term "Negro" should be removed from the questionnaire and the term "Black" substituted.

Tapes purchased from the Bureau of the Census should be ready for use without the need for additional time and effort to eliminate "bugs."

The State should designate one agency (within the State) to act as a clearing house for all information concerning census-data availability.

A total of 90 suggestions were made at the Phoenix meeting, and the process was repeated in dozens of other meetings around the country.

## INNOVATIONS

For the 1980 census, the Bureau made a major effort to improve the coverage of the Indian population. Involved in the effort were state governments, the Bureau of Indian Affairs, and tribal officials of each federal and state Indian reservation. Working with these groups, the Bureau compiled a list of 269 reservations for which 1980 census data was required. From the Bureau of Indian Affairs and from the various states came maps of legally recognized boundaries of the reservations. Tribal officials were then asked to review the maps of their reservations for accuracy.

Covering broader matters, a series of meetings were held with Indians around the country, culminating in a larger meeting at Washington, D.C., in 1978. Deputy Director of the Bureau Robert Hagan and six top-level officials met with Indian representatives from Alabama, Alaska, Connecticut, California, Oklahoma, Florida, and Virginia. Among concerns raised by the Indians was a fear that only "BIA Indians" (members of groups recognized by the Bureau of Indian Affairs) would be counted, and that many urban

Indians would not properly check the ancestry question on the questionnaire. Also voiced was the fear that Indians acknowledging residence on "trust lands" might somehow be discriminated against. Bureau officials promised to try to prevent such happenings.

## PRETESTS

"Pretesting" is an effective means of improving the procedures and the results of the census. As an example, in 1975 the Bureau attempted to upgrade its listing of rural addresses. Nine counties in Louisiana, Arkansas, and Mississippi were used as a test area, and several methods were compared:

1. "Knock when necessary." The enumerator uses his judgment of the situation and conducts an interview only when necessary.

2. "Knock on every door, no callbacks." The enumerator conducts an interview at every household to get address information. If a resident is not at home, the enumerator gets the address information from a neighbor and does not make another visit to that address.

3. "Knock on every door, with callbacks." The enumerator does call back if no one is home.

It was found that Method 2, "Knock on every door, no callbacks," was most effective, and this was the method was used in the 1980 census by rural enumerators.

All pretesting is not successful, however. In 1976, for example, careful pretesting was done in Gallia and Meigs counties, Ohio, to compare the use of a new type of basic geographic area called a Data Collection Unit, or DCU, with traditional enumeration districts. However, the DCU approach produced no reduction in missed units and it was decided to stay with traditional enumeration districts in 1980.

Pretests were also conducted in Travis County, Texas, and in Camden, New Jersey, in 1976, toward improving coverage of those who might otherwise be missed. Lists were obtained from local

CENSUS

community organizations, minority groups, departments of motor vehicles, and elsewhere. A comprehensive pretest was conducted in Oakland, California, in 1977, to improve data-collection techniques. Procedures included precanvassing as a means of reviewing the address lists used for the census, having local officials review the preliminary housing unit and population counts before they are released to the public, using Spanish-language questionnaires, checking to find if "vacant" households are truly vacant, and checking change-of-address information reported by the Postal Service to identify households that might otherwise be missed.

Evaluation of the Oakland pretest results led to the inclusion of more "race" categories in census questionnaires. Those included in 1980 were: white, black or Negro, Japanese, Chinese, Filipino, Korean, Vietnamese, Indian (American), Asian-Indian, Hawaiian, Guamanian, Samoan, Eskimo, Aleut, or "Other." Long-form questionnaires included a question on ancestry or ethnic origin. Ancestry groups included English, Polish, Afro-American, and so on. A question asking what language was spoken in the household was changed to require a response for all non-English languages, and the degree of their use in comparison with English.

Public information is an important factor in the success of a census, and much attention was given to this during the pretests in Travis County, Camden, and Oakland. For example, the Travis campaign material included brochures and flyers, newspaper, radio, and television advertising, and mobile-van-assistance units. Spanish-speaking viewers in San Antonio and Austin, Texas, received census information in that language. The Spanish-language TV station also conducted street interviews in conjuction with studio programming on the census. Flyers describing the census were given to children in the first through the sixth grade in Travis County and in Oakland. They also filled out a census questionnaire with a single question about age. After they completed the form they were encouraged to take it home to their parents. Just before "Census Day" on April 1, 1976, meetings were held with communications experts and local leaders to evaluate the effectiveness of the publicity campaign in Travis County.

Camden, New Jersey, posed more of a problem for publicity

efforts. The city gets it TV programming from Philadelphia, and Philadelphia newspapers cover Camden more effectively than does the local paper. To reach the black population, the Census Bureau used Philadelphia's "soul" stations, Community Service help, and printed material. The same techniques were used with Spanish-language newspapers and radio stations in Philadelphia to reach those of Spanish origin. Immediately following "Census Day," some 400 Camden residents were polled by direct interview to evaluate the effectiveness of the publicity campaign. Although this was a small sample, good correlation was reported between exposure to information about the pretest census and the completion and return of questionnaires.

## DRESS REHEARSALS

In addition to exhaustive pretesting, a "dress rehearsal" for the 1980 census was conducted in April, 1978. Richmond, Virginia, and the adjacent Virginia counties of Chesterfield and Henrico were covered by the mail-back system that is being used for most of the country in the real census. La Plata and Montezuma counties in southwest Colorado were covered by the door-to-door enumeration system used in 1980 for sparsely settled areas.

Because of its responsibility for many social and economic programs for American Indians on the reservation, the federal government requested additional data on these people from the Census Bureau. As part of the Colorado dress rehearsal, a supplementary questionnaire was included for all reservation Indians in the Ute Mountain and Southern Ute reservations. The results of the Colorado tests were carefully evaluated so that a similar Indian questionnaire could be used in the 1980 census, with the aim of providing 100 percent data on the Indian population. It was administered on a door-to-door basis, with questions about tribal affiliation, education, migration on and off reservation, health, labor force, income, and housing.

A special public-service publicity campaign for the Richmond dress rehearsal was conducted by the National Advertising Coun-

*Lively posters advertised a rehearsal for the 1970 census, held in Trenton, New Jersey.*

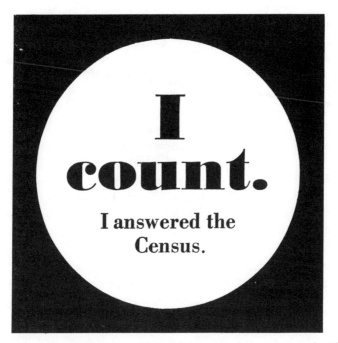

I count.

I answered the Census.

*Buttons were supplied to those helpful citizens who cooperated with the 1978 Colorado "dress rehearsal" census.*

cil, with the help of the New York advertising agency, Ogilvy & Mather, Inc., and the Pepsi-Cola Company.

Stickers saying "I count. I answered the Census," were distributed to spread the word, and radio spots urged a prompt mail-in. Explanatory news releases were put out both before and after "Census Day." The response was satisfactory, and the major problem that turned up was some confusion in responding to questions on ancestry. A new approach was designed for the final dress rehearsal.

## TROUBLE IN MANHATTAN

In September, 1978, a dress rehearsal census was taken in New York's Manhattan Borough south of Houston Street. This final dress rehearsal got off to a bad start. The date first scheduled was

September 12, but unfortunately that was also the date for the primary elections in New York. Congressmen took a dim view of the competition the census might represent, and the Census Bureau rescheduled the Manhattan dress rehearsal for September 26.

In 1912 the Census Bureau had used banners in San Francisco's Chinatown to convince residents the census would not be used to tax them or inconvenience them in any other way. In 1978 a much bigger public-relations campaign was waged in an attempt to get a good response from the Lower Manhattan area, which contained a Chinatown and much more, and was admittedly a very difficult place to enumerate. The area south of Houston Street has great ethnic variety and contains many low-income groups. Included are Greenwich Village and its mix, as well as the Chinese, blacks, Jews, Italians, and Puerto Ricans. Although other dress rehearsals had come out fairly well, it was not so in Lower Manhattan, and there were grim faces seen in many Census Bureau offices as experts sought to pinpoint the problems, and to find ways of fixing them before April 1, 1980.

*Lower Manhattan, with its great ethnic variety, challenged enumerators of the September 1978 "dress rehearsal" census.*

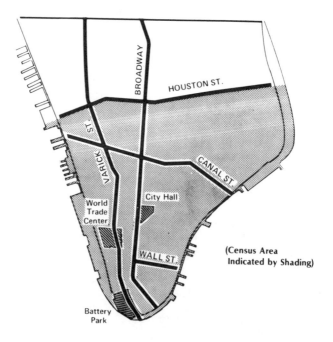

# CLOSING THE PEOPLE GAP

The 1970 census missed about 2.5 percent of the total population. Breaking it down by ethnic groups, only about 1.9 percent of white people were missed. But the miss rate for blacks was a sizable 7.7 percent. As the Bureau realizes, this undercount of a group can be a calamity in the slicing of that social, economic, and political pie. The "hard to enumerate" consist of several different segments of the population. There are those without a fixed place of residence, those living someplace where their presence may be questioned, those engaged in illegal activities, those who just don't want Uncle Sam to count them, and perhaps people in other categories as well.

Because the under-enumeration problem affects minorities more, the Census Bureau has made special efforts beyond those made in 1970. Three formal census advisory committees have been set up to represent blacks, people of Spanish origin, and Asian and Pacific Island Americans. A comparable effort has been made with the first Americans—the Indians. Another approach involves the newly established Community Services Program, minority representatives working for the Census Bureau who live in the areas involved. The Community Services concept got its start in 1970, when "community educators" numbering twenty or so were selected and given the task of communicating with the hard-to-enumerate populations of large cities. Although they were not typical Census workers, they were men and women who were accepted as leaders in the areas where they would be put to work for the census. For the 1980 effort the ranks of Community Services representatives was increased to about 200.

One solution often suggested for the undercount problem is a simple "adjustment." Why not just apply a correcting factor to population totals and thus come out with a more accurate count? Unfortunately, the Census Bureau fears that accurate adjustment criteria could be provided for only a few of the 39,000 or so entities receiving revenue-sharing funds. For example, there cound not be an adequate adjustment for Spanish-origin Americans in individual cities. The adjustment question is of such importance, however,

209

that the National Academy of Sciences Panel on Decennial Census Plans discussed it in its 1978 report. The Census Bureau also sponsored a conference of experts to study the problem in mid-1979.

## THE QUESTIONS

The "response burden" for the 1980 census was held to a minimum—no more than that for 1970, or even for 1960. As in 1970, all households received the short-form questionnaire containing only 19 simple questions. The average time it took to fill it out was about 15 minutes. For the 22 percent of households receiving the long form with 65 questions, the time came to about 45 minutes. In localities of less than 2,500 population, every other housing unit received the long form. Elsewhere, only 1 household in 6 did.

In a bow to changing times, the Bureau no longer used the term "head of household" in 1980. As the inevitable result of increasing "equal rights" demands, the Bureau first experimented with listing either a man or a woman as head of the house, instead of the traditional practice of listing a man. That did not work, however, and henceforth, or until it is changed again, households will be determined through a relationship question concerning the first person listed on the questionnaire.

In 1970, people of Spanish origin were identified on a 5-percent sample basis; in 1980 it was 100 percent. Further information on commuting patterns were requested in 1980, but vocational-training questions were deleted from the population questionnaire and questions about household appliances from the housing questionnaire. The disability question included in 1970 proved of little value, and much debate went into its inclusion in 1980. The options boiled down to: drop the question or continue to collect and present data of dubious quality in the absence of anything better. Another question that posed problems was the identification of substandard housing. In the past such questions have been ridiculed for their vagueness. New questions were used in the Oakland pretest, and also in the 1978 dress rehearsals.

The 1980 questionnaires were adjusted through the 1978 dress

*Finishing touches are applied to the master copy of the 1980 census questionnaire. More than 150 million of these forms have been printed.*

rehearsals, with changes made as necessary from field testing. By January, 1979, the questionnaire was "locked up" and sent to the printer. The following are the questions that were included in the two forms.

### 1980 CENSUS DATA COLLECTION ITEMS
*(Regular Census Questionnaire)*

### 100-PERCENT ITEMS

*Population*

Household relationship
Sex
Race
Age
Marital status
Spanish origin or descent

*Housing*

Number of units in structure
Complete plumbing facilities
Number of rooms
Tenure (whether the unit is owned or rented)
Cooperative/condominium identification

211

Value of home (for owner-occupied
  units and condominiums)
Rent (for renter-occupied units)
Vacant for rent, for sale, etc.; and
  period of vacancy

Industry
Occupation
Class of worker
Time worked in 1979
Amount of income by source and total
  income in 1979

### SAMPLE ITEMS

*Population*

School enrollment
Educational attainment
State of birth
Citizenship and year of immigration
Ancestry
Current language
Year moved into this house
Place of residence five years ago
Major activity five years ago
Veteran status
Presence of disability or handicap
Children ever born
Date of first marriage and whether
  terminated by death
Employment status
Hours worked last week (for employed
  persons)
Place of work
Time duration of journey to work
Means of transportation to work
Carpool participation
Whether looking for work (for unem-
  ployed persons)

*Housing*

Stories in building and presence of an
  elevator
Year built
Acreage and farm residence
Source of water
Sewage disposal
Heating equipment
Fuels used for house heating, water
  heating, and cooking
Costs of fuels and utilities
Complete kitchen facilities
Number of bedrooms
Number of bathrooms
Existence of specific structural defi-
  ciencies or damage
Telephone
Air conditioning
Number of automobiles
Number of light trucks and vans
Homeowner shelter costs for mort-
  gage, real estate taxes, and hazard
  insurance
Existence of property improvement
  loan

## TAKING THE CENSUS

Any army involved in a long-range campaign has a timetable it must adhere to, and Census 1980 is no exception:

## KEY DATES

| | |
|---|---|
| March 31, 1978 | Transmittal of a list of specific questions planned for the 1980 census to Congress (Required by Title 13, U.S. Code). |
| April 4, 1978 | Dress rehearsal censuses in Richmond and La Plata and Montezuma Counties, Colorado. |
| May 1, 1978 | Completion of publication specifications for 100-percent data (subject to revision). |
| September 26, 1978 | Dress rehearsal census in Lower Manhattan, New York City. |
| October 15, 1978 | Completion of publication specifications for sample data for small areas. |
| January 1, 1979 | Census questionnaires to printer. |
| March 15, 1979 | Completion of publication specifications for sample data for large areas. |
| July, 1979 | Community Services Program fully staffed. |
| April, 1979–January, 1980 | Assemble and address 86 million questionnaire mailing pieces. |
| January, 1980 | Open 409 temporary field district offices. |
| January–February 1980 | Review of pre-enumeration/housing counts by local authorities. |
| February–March 1980 | Special precanvass field check of addresses in city areas. |
| March 6, 1980 | Questionnaire mailing pieces received by local post offices for predelivery check. |
| March 28, 1980 | Questionnaires delivered by postal carriers to all households. |
| April 1, 1980 | Census Day! |

213

# CENSUS BY MAIL

There was a postal system in America at the time of the 1790 census, but it was used only for carrying results from the states to New York. In 1980, Uncle Sam's mail carriers are handling even more questionnaires than the 60-percent effort of 1970. Only sparsely settled areas such as Alaska, some sections of the Rocky Mountains, and some in the Southwestern States, are being covered by the legendary census taker, afoot or astride whatever vehicle best suits the terrain and other conditions. Those who don't mail back their questionnaires receive a follow-up visit from a flesh-and-blood representative of the Census Bureau. Those who mail back incomplete questionnaires receive either a telephone follow-up or a personal visit from a census taker.

This further shift away from the traditional pavement-pounding, trail-riding, indomitable enumerators of old may be hard on legends, but it is appreciated by those who don't relish the rebuffs and other hazards associated with personal census taking. It is also appreciated by the Census Bureau, which points to the 87 percent return of questionnaires in 1970. In the 1978 dress rehearsal in Richmond, Virginia, the mail-return rate was an encouraging 78 percent.

As census taking swung into action on April 1, Bureau officials had two key dates burned in their minds: January 1 and April 1, 1981. The first order of business is the "100-percent data capture and tabulation." By law, the Census Bureau must provide the President of the United States with that final official population counts and the reapportionment of the House of Representatives by January 1, 1981. This is a much harder job than it may seem, for it takes some temporary district offices about three months after Census Day to complete their work. This leaves the Bureau just five months to carry out its responsibility.

To add to the problem, new legislation now makes it mandatory that the Bureau also provide each state with a geographically detailed population count for redistricting purposes by April 1, 1981, just a year after Census Day, 1980. This second milestone is not simply a total population count; it must accurately cover the more than 2.5 million city blocks recognized in the 1980 census.

# PROCESSING THE INFORMATION

To busy Bureau personnel it must seem that the actual enumeration process will never be complete, and in a sense the counting is never completely done. But the time does eventually come when "Enough!" is called and the 1980 census moves on to another difficult phase.

The sheer physical volume of data produced by the 280,000-person census army is enough to chill the heart of the most capable data processor. In 1970, far fewer enumerators produced 250 boxcars of questionnaires, and a total of about 200 million forms were photographed on 180,000 rolls of microfilm. This greatly reduced volume of data was then further shrunk through FOSDIC machines to 18,000 reels of computer tape holding some 4 billion bits of information.

Because of the additional amount of work in processing census questionnaires in 1980, the Census Bureau put two new facilities into operation. One is the Michoud Assembly Facility in New Orleans, the other a new federal building at Laguna Niguel in California.

The Michoud Plant, which served recently in the assembly of spacecraft for NASA, was used during World War II for the production of ships and aircraft. In 1978 some 1,500 Census personnel began gearing up to process 25 million of the 86 million household questionnaires that were produced in April of 1980. Practice toward that goal was gained in processing questionnaires from the 1978 dress rehearsal censuses.

The second facility to be added for the 1980 census processing effort is a handsome new federal building at Laguna Niguel, midway between Los Angeles and San Diego. Like the Michoud facility, Laguna Niguel will employ about 1,500 temporary workers and process 25 million questionnaires.

For the 1980 effort the Bureau is using 60 microfilming units and 12 FOSDIC-80 readers. FOSDIC's track record includes not only its brilliant performance in the 1970 American census, but service in the Canadian censuses of 1971 and 1976 as well. This is comforting to the hard-pressed technicians who must convert a billion or so pages of questionnaires into more billions of invisible magnetic

215

blips on many miles of computer tapes. It should also qualify the machine for the name "Fearless FOSDIC."

Microfilming crews work two shifts, six days a week. FOSDIC readers operate around the clock until their work is done and all reels of tape are safely canned and ready for the next step in the census process: running the high-speed computers that tabulate billions of pieces of information and produce the many publications representing that information.

Computer-programming problems caused delays and cost money in the 1970 processing runs. For 1980, the Bureau has spent much time in getting subject analysts and computer programmers on the same wavelength. This is accomplished by using standardized glossaries. Computers were switched from machine languages to "higher-order" languages; this requires more computer time but prevents some of the problems experienced in 1970.

Traditionally the Bureau has guarded the confidentiality of census data by using "suppression techniques" in handling it. This safeguards individual information in published statistics. As usual, no good deed goes unpunished, however, and many users complain that the suppression of small blocks of information also suppresses useful information (for marketing or other business purposes) that might come from them. Yielding to pressure from individual users and task-force groups, the Bureau is taking a second look at its traditional procedures.

It turns out that suppression of information may not be the foolproof protector of privacy it was thought to be. To guarantee confidentiality absolutely requires such rigid suppression measures that most of the information is made useless or nearly so. Bureau experts have been looking at Canadian and European statistical techniques, and it now seems that there may be workable alternatives to traditional suppression techniques. It will be interesting to see what kind of compromise or accommodation is worked out in the future.

## PRODUCTS OF THE CENSUS

What the Bureau calls a "first count" is the initial tabulation of enumeration results. First-count tapes are available at the end of the census year. The "second count" is a more exhaustive tabulation of census data, including race, sex, age, and relationship to the head of household. Second-count tapes are completed by the spring of the year following the census. The "third count" is primarily a tabulation of housing characteristics by blocks. The "fourth count" contains some 1,200 groups of data covering ethnic characteristics, mobility, education, families, labor force, occupation and industry, income, and more. Complete fourth-count tapes and printouts for smaller areas are available in the spring and summer of the year following the census.

Next is the printout of census tracts, some 35,000 in all. These are reports about age, sex, family relationship, country of origin, school enrollment, years of school completed, migration, place of work and means of transportation, labor force, occupation and industry, class of worker, income, and characteristics of low-income families.

In the "fifth count," enumeration district and block group data similar to that in Census Tract reports are tallied and consolidated to Zip Code areas. Data will be available on tape at the 5-digit level for metropolitan areas and at the 3-digit level on a nationwide basis.

In addition to 2,000 computer tapes, census data is available on "microfiche," 4- by 6-inch cards containing 70 pages of printed material that can be magnified on special readers. About 1,600 Census Bureau reports can be purchased in this form from the National Technical Information Service.

The Census Bureau in 1970 published some 2,000 printed reports in 27 different series of publications. These totaled about 200,000 pages, plus an additional 75,000 pages in a set of 59 hardcover volumes containing material reprinted from the basic reports. In 1980 there will be an estimated 250,000 pages. To do this massive publishing job in the short time allotted to it, the Bureau relies on sophisticated computer printing systems that produce 1,200 characters of composed copy a second and complete a page of census data in an average of 20 seconds. Federal Building Number 4 at Suitland houses the extensive publications operations of the Bureau.

*A census researcher reviews statistical data for one of the many publications produced by the Bureau.*

## SUMMARY

The 1980 census is scheduled to end officially in June, 1983, at which time everything, including final publication of thousands of reports, must be complete and ready for distribution. On that

Please fill out this
official Census Form
and mail it back on
Census Day,
Tuesday, April 1, 1980

# 1980
# Census of the
# United States

| DO | A1 | A2 | A4 | A5 S | A6 |
|----|----|----|----|------|-----|

A message from the Director,
Bureau of the Census . . .

We must, from time to time, take stock of ourselves as a people if our Nation is to meet successfully the many national and local challenges we face. This is the purpose of the 1980 census.

The essential need for a population census was recognized almost 200 years ago when our Constitution was written. As provided by article I, the first census was conducted in 1790 and one has been taken every 10 years since then.

The law under which the census is taken protects the confidentiality of your answers. For the next 72 years — or until April 1, 2052 — only sworn census workers have access to the individual records, and no one else may see them.

Your answers, when combined with the answers from other people, will provide the statistical figures needed by public and private groups, schools, business and industry, and Federal, State, and local governments across the country. These figures will help all sectors of American society understand how our population and housing are changing. In this way, we can deal more effectively with today's problems and work toward a better future for all of us.

Your answers are confidential

By law (title 13, U.S. Code), census employees are subject to fine and/or imprisonment for any disclosure of your answers. Only after 72 years does your information become available to other government agencies or the public. The same law requires that you answer the questions to the best of your knowledge.

The census is a vitally important national activity. Please do your part by filling out this census form accurately and completely. If you mail it back promptly in the enclosed postage-paid envelope, it will save the expense and inconvenience of a census taker having to visit you.

Thank you for your cooperation.

Para personas de habla hispana

(For Spanish-speaking persons):
SI USTED DESEA UN CUESTIONARIO DEL CENSO EN ESPAÑOL llame a la oficina del censo. El número de teléfono se encuentra en el encasillado de la dirección.

O, si prefiere, marque esta casilla ☐ y devuelva el cuestionario por correo en el sobre que se le incluye.

U.S. Department of Commerce
Bureau of the Census
Form D-1

Form Approved:
O.M.B. No. 41-S78006

Please continue ➚

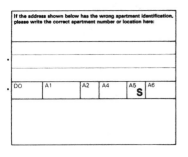

*The 1980 form, as it will be answered by millions of Americans of every age, race, educational background, and other statistics.*

219

**→ ALSO ANSWER THE HOUSING QUESTION**

| Here are the QUESTIONS ↓ | These are the columns for ANSWERS → | PERSON in column 1 | PERSON in column 2 | |
|---|---|---|---|---|
| | Please fill one column for each person listed in Question 1. | Last name / First name — Middle initial | Last name / First name — Middle initial | Last name / First name |
| **2. How is this person related to the person in column 1?** *Fill one circle.* If "Other relative" of person in column 1, give exact relationship, such as mother-in-law, niece, grandson, etc. | | *START in this column with the household member (or one of the members) in whose name the home is owned or rented. If there is no such person, start in this column with any adult household member.* | If relative of person in column 1: ○ Husband/wife  ○ Father/mother  ○ Son/daughter  ○ Other relative —  ○ Brother/sister  If not related to person in column 1: ○ Roomer, boarder  ○ Other nonrelative  ○ Partner, roommate  ○ Paid employee | If relative ○ Hu ○ Sc ○ Br If not relat ○ Ro ○ Pa ○ Pa |
| **3. Sex** *Fill one circle.* | | ○ Male  ■  ○ Female | ○ Male  ■  ○ Female | ○ M |
| **4. Is this person —** *Fill one circle.* | | ○ White  ○ Asian Indian  ○ Black or Negro  ○ Hawaiian  ○ Japanese  ○ Guamanian  ○ Chinese  ○ Samoan  ○ Filipino  ○ Eskimo  ○ Korean  ○ Aleut  ○ Vietnamese  ○ Other — *Specify*  ○ Indian (Amer.) *Print tribe* | ○ White  ○ Asian Indian  ○ Black or Negro  ○ Hawaiian  ○ Japanese  ○ Guamanian  ○ Chinese  ○ Samoan  ○ Filipino  ○ Eskimo  ○ Korean  ○ Aleut  ○ Vietnamese  ○ Other — *Specify*  ○ Indian (Amer.) *Print tribe* | ○ Wl ○ Bl ○ Ja ○ Ch ○ Fil ○ Kc ○ Vil ○ Inc |
| **5. Age, and month and year of birth** *a. Print age at last birthday.* *b. Print month and fill one circle.* *c. Print year in the spaces, and fill one circle below each number.* | | a. Age at last birthday   c. Year of birth *1* 1 ● 8 ○ 0 ○ 0 ○  9 ○ 1 ○ 1 ○  b. Month of birth   2 ○ 2 ○  3 ○ 3 ○  4 ○ 4 ○  ○ Jan.—Mar.  5 ○ 5 ○  ○ Apr.—June  6 ○ 6 ○  7 ○ 7 ○  ○ July—Sept.  8 ○ 8 ○  9 ○ 9 ○  ○ Oct.—Dec. | a. Age at last birthday   c. Year of birth *1* 1 ● 8 ○ 0 ○ 0 ○  9 ○ 1 ○ 1 ○  b. Month of birth   2 ○ 2 ○  3 ○ 3 ○  4 ○ 4 ○  ○ Jan.—Mar.  5 ○ 5 ○  ○ Apr.—June  6 ○ 6 ○  7 ○ 7 ○  ○ July—Sept.  8 ○ 8 ○  9 ○ 9 ○  ○ Oct.—Dec. | a. Age at birthda b. Month birth ○ Ja ○ Ap ○ Ju ○ Oc |
| **6. Marital status** *Fill one circle.* | | ○ Now married  ○ Separated  ○ Widowed  ○ Never married  ○ Divorced | ○ Now married  ○ Separated  ○ Widowed  ○ Never married  ○ Divorced | ○ Nc ○ W ○ Di |
| **7. Is this person of Spanish/Hispanic origin or descent?** *Fill one circle.* | | ○ No (not Spanish/Hispanic)  ○ Yes, Mexican, Mexican-Amer., Chicano  ○ Yes, Puerto Rican  ○ Yes, Cuban ■  ○ Yes, other Spanish/Hispanic | ○ No (not Spanish/Hispanic)  ○ Yes, Mexican, Mexican-Amer., Chicano  ○ Yes, Puerto Rican  ○ Yes, Cuban ■  ○ Yes, other Spanish/Hispanic | ○ Ne ○ Ye ○ Ye ○ Ye ○ Ye |
| | | CENSUS USE ONLY  **A.**  ○ I  ○ N  ○ O | CENSUS USE ONLY  **A.**  ○ I  ○ N  ○ O | CENSUS USE ONL |

| PERSON in column 4 | PERSON in column 5 | PERSON in column 6 |
|---|---|---|
| Last name | Last name | Last name |
| First name / Middle initial | First name / Middle initial | First name / Middle initial |

**If relative of person in column 1:**

| Column 4 | Column 5 | Column 6 |
|---|---|---|
| ○ Husband/wife  ○ Father/mother | ○ Husband/wife  ○ Father/mother | ○ Husband/wife  ○ Father/mother |
| ○ Son/daughter  ○ Other relative | ○ Son/daughter  ○ Other relative | ○ Son/daughter  ○ Other relative |
| ○ Brother/sister | ○ Brother/sister | ○ Brother/sister |

**If not related to person in column 1:**

| Column 4 | Column 5 | Column 6 |
|---|---|---|
| ○ Roomer, boarder  ○ Other nonrelative | ○ Roomer, boarder  ○ Other nonrelative | ○ Roomer, boarder  ○ Other nonrelative |
| ○ Partner, roommate | ○ Partner, roommate | ○ Partner, roommate |
| ○ Paid employee | ○ Paid employee | ○ Paid employee |

| ○ Male  ■  ○ Female | ○ Male  ■  ○ Female | ○ Male  ■  ○ Female |
|---|---|---|

| Column 4 | Column 5 | Column 6 |
|---|---|---|
| ○ White  ○ Asian Indian | ○ White  ○ Asian Indian | ○ White  ○ Asian Indian |
| ○ Black or Negro  ○ Hawaiian | ○ Black or Negro  ○ Hawaiian | ○ Black or Negro  ○ Hawaiian |
| ○ Japanese  ○ Guamanian | ○ Japanese  ○ Guamanian | ○ Japanese  ○ Guamanian |
| ○ Chinese  ○ Samoan | ○ Chinese  ○ Samoan | ○ Chinese  ○ Samoan |
| ○ Filipino  ○ Eskimo | ○ Filipino  ○ Eskimo | ○ Filipino  ○ Eskimo |
| ○ Korean  ○ Aleut | ○ Korean  ○ Aleut | ○ Korean  ○ Aleut |
| ○ Vietnamese  ○ Other — Specify | ○ Vietnamese  ○ Other — Specify | ○ Vietnamese  ○ Other — Specify |
| ○ Indian (Amer.) Print tribe | ○ Indian (Amer.) Print tribe | ○ Indian (Amer.) Print tribe |

**a. Age at last birthday  c. Year of birth  b. Month of birth**

| Column 4 | Column 5 | Column 6 |
|---|---|---|
| ○ Jan.—Mar. | ○ Jan.—Mar. | ○ Jan.—Mar. |
| ○ Apr.—June | ○ Apr.—June | ○ Apr.—June |
| ○ July—Sept. | ○ July—Sept. | ○ July—Sept. |
| ○ Oct.—Dec. | ○ Oct.—Dec. | ○ Oct.—Dec. |

| Column 4 | Column 5 | Column 6 |
|---|---|---|
| ○ Now married  ○ Separated | ○ Now married  ○ Separated | ○ Now married  ○ Separated |
| ○ Widowed  ○ Never married | ○ Widowed  ○ Never married | ○ Widowed  ○ Never married |
| ○ Divorced | ○ Divorced | ○ Divorced |

| Column 4 | Column 5 | Column 6 |
|---|---|---|
| ○ No (not Spanish/Hispanic) | ○ No (not Spanish/Hispanic) | ○ No (not Spanish/Hispanic) |
| ○ Yes, Mexican, Mexican-Amer., Chicano | ○ Yes, Mexican, Mexican-Amer., Chicano | ○ Yes, Mexican, Mexican-Amer., Chicano |
| ○ Yes, Puerto Rican | ○ Yes, Puerto Rican | ○ Yes, Puerto Rican |
| ○ Yes, Cuban | ○ Yes, Cuban | ○ Yes, Cuban |
| ○ Yes, other Spanish/Hispanic | ○ Yes, other Spanish/Hispanic | ○ Yes, other Spanish/Hispanic |

| CENSUS USE ONLY  A. ○ I  ○ N  ○○ | CENSUS USE ONLY  A. ○ I  ○ N  ○○ | CENSUS USE ONLY  A. ○ I  ○ N  ○○ |
|---|---|---|

happy date, the Director of the Bureau and his colleagues can breathe a brief sigh of satisfaction as the last report comes off the press, and then get busy on the first mid-decade census coming in 1985.

# 12
# The Census Tomorrow

Having been burned a time or two, the Bureau of the Census is understandably cautious in predicting future population or future anything else. However, the future of the Bureau itself seems one of increasing growth, with little prospect of leveling off. Indeed, the explosion of census-data use suggests a much greater role for the Bureau in the years ahead. Government and business depend more and more on census-generated population data; the first order of business in the Bureau's busy future will be gathering and presenting that data every five years instead of ten.

## THE MID-DECADE CENSUS

The future stems largely from the past, and the 5-year census is no exception; the first President to request such an enumeration was Ulysses S. Grant, in 1872. Two years later, General Francis A. Walker, Superintendent of the Census, urged it again, and Secretary of the Interior Columbus Delano added his support. The idea's time had not yet come, however, and the Congress balked at ordering the counting of humans twice as often as the Constitution had decreed.

Almost a century after President Grant's request, something happened at last to speed action toward a 5-year census. In 1964, the U.S. Supreme Court ruled that the "one-man, one-vote" philosophy must govern legislative apportionments. Under the gun to redistrict in line with this order, the states were hampered by population figures already half a decade old; Congress responded in 1965 by introducing a bill for a special census in 1966 to provide up-to-date statistics for reshaping state legislatures.

Witnesses who testified favorably at hearings on the bill included senators and representatives, mayors, governors, and businessmen. Their reasons were sound and their testimony eloquent, but the push had come too quickly. There was so much counsel against being stampeded in the heat of the one-man, one-vote edict that the bill died. However, in 1967 a new bill was introduced, ordering not just a special census but a continuing series of censuses to be held in years ending in "5," thus halving the time between population counts.

Arguments were even more eloquent than in 1965. Congressman Morris Udall of Arizona pointed out that annual federal revenue-sharing funds had already jumped from the $8 billion figure he had cited earlier to $13 billion, emphasizing the need for up-to-date statistics to ensure fair allocations. (Today's revenue-sharing money is about $50 billion.) Another strong argument came from Dr. A. Ross Eckler, Director of the Bureau of the Census. Eckler pointed to Bureau estimates that about 20 million people counted in the 1960 census were living in a different state by 1967, and that more than half the population had moved at least once to a new residence.

Train travelers of old complained that when they reached Chicago they had to change railroads to continue their journey but that pigs riding in freight cars went straight through. Senator Robert Byrd of West Virginia used a similar porcine precedent in his testimony at the 1967 hearings on the mid-decade census:

Mr. President, the other day I had need to know the population of my State, West Virginia; so I called the Census Bureau. They told me West Virginia's population in 1960 was 1,860,421. But 1960 was seven years ago, and I was interested in the population today, or as close to today as possible. The Census Bureau people told me they estimate the population as of last July at 1,794,000. . . .
As a matter of curiosity, I inquired how many pigs there are in the State—and how often they are counted. I learned that the pigs were counted at the end of 1964, and at the end of 1959, just 5 years apart. The pig population in 1959 had been 148,238, and 5 years later it had dropped to 77,791.
The Census Bureau counts pigs every 5 years—but counts people only once in 10 years. This is the timetable established—not by the Bureau of the Census, but by Congress. If it seems to represent a distorted sense of values—that pigs should be counted twice as often as people—let us not look elsewhere to point the finger of blame. The timetable is established here, in Congress.

Even this finger-pointing was not immediately successful; although the House of Representatives passed a 5-year census bill in 1967, the Senate took no action on it. Only in 1976 was President Grant answered at last. On October 17 of that year President Ford signed Public Law 94–521, amending Title 13 of the United States to provide for a mid-decade census:

Without regard to subsections (a), (b), and (c) of this section, the Secretary [of Commerce], in the year 1985 and every 10 years thereafter, shall conduct a mid-decade census of population in such form and content as he may determine, including the use of sampling procedures and special surveys, taking into account the extent to which information to be obtained from the such census will serve in lieu of information collected annually or less frequently in surveys or other statistical studies. The census shall be taken as of the first of April of each such year, which date shall be known as the "mid-decade census date."

Accustomed to the "decennial" census, some observers began speaking of the coming "quinquennial," or 5-year, census. However, the mid-decade effort will also be a 10-year, or "decennial," census, taken once every 10 years in the year ending in 5. Whether or not the decennial and mid-decade efforts will one day merge into a true quinquennial census remains to be seen.

The new law not only authorized a mid-decade census but also strengthened confidentiality provisions for census and survey records, and it removed the jail penalty for refusal to answer mandatory censuses and surveys. Reflecting the continuing objections by many to disclose their religious preference, the new law also contained a provision that no person shall be required to disclose information regarding religious belief or affiliation.

Congress intentionally did not spell out the scope and content of the 5-year census. Instead, the legislation is written flexibly enough to allow the Secretary of Commerce to decide what information is needed in 1985. Neither did Congress intend that the mid-decade census duplicate the decennial census or be used in apportioning the House of Representatives or changing congressional districts. In fact, the law prohibits such use.

The Census Bureau has not yet committed itself to detailed plans or methods for taking the 1985 census. Three years before the census it must report to the Congress on subjects to be covered, and two years before it remits the questions to be asked. The basic philosophy most probably will be the same that has prevailed in shaping the 10-year censuses: providing a valid data base for decision makers in government and business.

## DIDD, THE PICTURE WORTH A THOUSAND WORDS

Beyond the 1985 census, the future is less clear. However, there probably will be changes not only in the frequency of counts but in the methods of presenting the information. As our population moves toward a quarter of a billion, and our social, political, and economic lives become increasingly complex, information must be refined in detail and speed of presentation to be useful for *planning* the American future instead of belatedly *reacting* to it after it happens.

In 1978, some of the young blood in the Carter Administration did something about the problem. The technique they used was called Domestic Information Display Demonstration (DIDD). The idea was simple: for administrative decision making, the young analysts wanted a data base common to all users, speedy access to that information, and easy methods of using it. Billions of pieces of information available in Census Bureau documents and tapes form a valid data base, and electronic displays can present the information in a form more comprehensible than text or tables.

Richard Harden, President Carter's Director of Administration and Information Management, was tired of sitting around for weeks waiting for a presentation of available statistics—a time delay that often made the presentation useless by the time it could be formulated. Enlisting help from the Census Bureau, the Library of Congress, and the U.S. Senate, Harden also brought NASA into the project for its computer-mapping and communications capabilities.

During a hectic April and May in 1978, the fledgling DIDD project was put together. Joined by communication links from NASA's Goddard Space Flight Center at Greenbelt, Maryland, and a downtown video microwave link, were the Capitol and the White House. The underlying concept was "A picture is worth a thousand words." The secret was not so much in the data, which had always been there, but in the manner in which it was presented: on a 6-foot video computer presentation—in living color.

The census data used 256 items, including population, education, labor, families, housing, voting, finances, manufacturing, retail trade, agriculture, and hospitals, and they could be displayed graphically, in color, and at various geographical levels, such as the nation at the county level, the states at the county level, and SMSAs at the Census Tract level. DIDD was set up as an "interactive" system that presented "menus" for the data user to choose from. For example, should the user pick Item 3 from "Menu 1," Item 5 from "Menu 2," and Item 8 from "Menu 3," the video screen would display a color-coded computer map for unemployment in the Detroit Standard Metropolitan Statistical Area.

Another typical scenario presented employment at the national level and compared it with employment in Iowa. A third fast-action study printed out the urban population in Florida, the percentage of persons with 4 years of high school, and the number of persons below the poverty level—all on colored computer maps for easy comparison.

In using the DIDD system, a user could choose the desired geographical area, select from the 256 items, combine items, modify the statistical limits, select the type of presentation for statistics, enlarge the area of interest by "zooming" the video screen, sequence the resulting images, and change colors as desired.

The DIDD presentation was impressive. It included such scenarios as the continuing population flight to "sunbelt" states, and information about the Proposition 13 tax revolt in California. The long-range hope is that patterns or trends can be detected quickly enough for something to be done about crime, unemployment, government spending, and a host of other problems.

*Time* magazine covered the DIDD happening and ended its report with a fanciful projection of its future:

> . . . Hamilton Jordan in a domestic command bunker, farm boots up on the computer console, phone in hand, lights flashing across huge screens: "Get Strauss out to Pittsburgh, the steel areas are angry red. . . . Tell Califano to shut up on tobacco, North Carolina has dropped off the map. . . . Can Brown pump some defense contracts into the East Coast? Unemployment is edging up. For God's sake, is Bergland loose again? Kansas is turning blue. . . ."

There are two ways of assessing the DIDD prospect. The "Nipkow disc," a forerunner of TV, was a crude visual demonstration on a par with a hand-cranked penny-arcade movie. But it triggered a media revolution, and TV is now a mighty force in our lives. Computer-mapped census data might be a similar breakthrough, or be as disappointing as the lack of improvement in weather prediction despite such developments as the Global Orbiting Environmental Satellite. Even looking at the weather as it happens all over the world, meteorologists seem to do little better than in the old days of piecemeal weather prognostication. Furthermore, sociology, politics, and economics tend to be less scientific than is meteorology. We will just have to wait and see how effective such approaches as DIDD can be.

# THE CENSUS IN THE FUTURE

High on the list of priorities for future census efforts will surely be the reduction of population undercounts, particularly of minority groups. The time will come, however, when the Bureau can do no better. That last percentage point or so of population may remain forever unaccountable, just as science can never achieve a perfect vacuum or a temperature of absolute zero, no matter how big its pumps or how good its insulation.

More success will likely be achieved in the faster reporting of information. The mail-out, mail-back census was a breakthrough; there will be others in future census taking. It has long been suggested that voting, and periodic public polls on topical issues, could be conducted with feedback from TV sets in people's homes. Perhaps the census will be taken this way in the year 2000.

The time may also come when no census count as such will be necessary. When all the great information links are in and operating in both directions, population, finances, transportation, business, industry, and education may report themselves without human help—or hindrance. Some future eye-in-the-sky may measure the nation's activity as it happens and automatically put into motion the corrective feedbacks necessary to achieve desired goals.

Predicting the future is as iffy as attempting to estimate the number of humans who will share that future. Has the process of living really become so complex that government and business need to know almost every tiny aspect of it? The simple life our ancestors knew in 1790 seems gone forever. Not even the most enthusiastic planner of that census could have dreamed that in half a dozen generations we could cram onto a computer tape the vital statistics and much else about all our hundreds of millions of Americans, and then, with the push of a button, spill out all those facts in nearly any conceivable form and for any conceivable purpose!

What does seem fairly safe to predict is that there will be a Bureau of the Census or some equivalent in our future to mirror our people, gauge our economy, and measure our land. For man, after all, is the counting animal.

229

# Abbreviations Used in This Book

| | |
|---|---|
| ADMATCH | Address Matching |
| AID | Agency for International Development |
| BG | Block Group |
| CARPOL | Carpooling |
| CATI | Computer-Assisted Telephone Interviewing |
| CBD | Central Business District |
| CCD | Census Counting Division |
| CT | Census Tract |
| DCU | Data Collection Unit |
| DIMECO | Dual Independent Map Encoding |
| DUSD | Data User Services Division |
| ED | Enumeration Districts |
| FOSDIC | Film Optical Scanning Device for Input to Computers |
| GBF/DIME | Geographical Base Files/Dual Independent Map Encoding |
| GNP | Gross National Product |
| MCD | Minor Civil Division |

MRC       Major Retail Center
SMSA     Standard Metropolitan Statistical Area
UA        Urban Area
UNIMATCH  Universal Matching
USES     Unified Statistical Evaluation Study
ZIPMATCH  Zip Coding
ZPG      Zero Population Growth

# Additional Reading

Alterman, Hyman. *Counting People: The Census as History.* New York: Harcourt, Brace, Jovanovich, 1969.

Anderson, Madelyn K. *The Census.* New York: Vanguard, 1979.

Holt, William S. *The Bureau of the Census: Its History, Activities, and Organization.* Washington, D.C.: Brookings Institution, reprint of 1929 edition.

*National Censuses and the United Nations.* New York: Unipub, 1977.

Scott, Ann Herbert. *Census, U.S.A.: Fact Finding for the American People, 1790–1970.* New York: Seabury Press, 1968.

Titles by the Census Bureau are available through the U.S. Government Printing Office's retail bookstores, located throughout the country. For a list of these bookstores, write to:

U.S. Government Printing Office
710 North Capitol Street
Washington, D.C. 20402

The following selected reference publications from the Census Bureau may be of particular interest:
*Bureau of the Census Catalog*
*Bureau of the Census Catalog of Publications, 1790–1970*
*Bureau of the Census Guide to Programs and Publications*
*Data User News* (monthly)
*Mini-Guide to the 1972 Economic Censuses*
*Reference Manual to Population and Housing Statistics*

The selected statistical compendia listed below may also be the source of valuable census information:
*Statistical Abstract of the United States* (annual)
*Pocket Data Book, USA* (biennial)
*County and City Data Book* (quinquennial)
*Congressional District Data Book*
*Historical Statistics of the United States, Colonial Times to 1970*

# Index

234

# Index

237

storage, methods of, 14
suppression and confidentiality, 216
use, 178
variety of, 96
Insurance rate tables, first, 26
International
    Business Machine company and census
        counting device, 48
    Statistical Programs Center, 63
Ireland, first census of, 25
Italy, first true census in, 27

Japanese-Americans, confidentiality
    about, 150
Jefferson, Thomas, as first census head, 33
Jeffersonville, Indiana, processing center,
    68
Jesus and Roman census, 20

Kennedy, Joseph, C.S., and 1860 census,
    42

Labor Statistics, Bureau of, data needed
    by, 167
Laguna Niguel Assembly Facility, 215
Land, Measurement of the, 97
Law, laws
    Enforcement Assistance
        Administration, help for, 94
    for five-year census, 225
    immigration, effect of, 78
Lawsuits and the census, 149
Library, Census, resources of, 66
Life-styles, changes in, 77
Locations
    reaching difficult, 158
    surveyed, 157

Machiavelli, Niccolo
    as census analyst, 24
    and Portraits of France and Germany,
        24
Madison, James, and census ideas, 32
Mail questionnaires, 50, 57, 196, 214, 215
Major Retail Centers, 104, 105
Malthus, Thomas, and population theory,
    26, 131
Manufactures
    Annual Survey of, 120
    Census of, 119, 120
    Census of in 1810, 39
Mapping by computers, 182
Maps, use of, 105
Marketing research and census data, 13,
    183, 191
Measurement of the land, 97
Medicare Survey, data of, 67

Men to women, ratios of, 83
Methods of census taking, 9, 55, 171
Metropolitan Map Series, 105
Microfiche, data on, 218
Michoud Assembly Facility, 215
Mid-decade census. See Five-year census.
Military data, 113
Minor Civil Divisions, 104
Minority, minorities. See also Ethnic,
    Names of specific groups.
    programs of Bureau of Census, 64
    underenumeration of, 12, 75, 209
Minsk-32 computers, 57
Mission of census, 62
Missing rate on population. See
    Underenumeration.
Mobility of Americans, 89
Moriarity, Joseph, and census legal case,
    149

Names in first census, 37
National
    Archives, record storage in, 153
    Crime Panel, 93, 94
    Data Bank, opposition to, 144
    Technical Information Service, reports
        from, 217
"Natural and Political Observations . . .
    made upon the Bills of Mortality," 25
Necker, Jacques, and statistical sampling,
    22
Norway, first census in, 27

Occupations surveyed, 162
Offenses and Penalties for failure to ans-
    wer, 144
Offices
    regional. See Regional offices.
    temporary, 171
Opposition to census, 11, 26, 59, 139, 143

Penalties
    for confidentiality breach, 143
    for failure to answer, 33, 144
    for refusal to answer, removal of, 226
Period, census, 200
Personal
    access to census records, 14
    Census Service Branch, 14, 68
    Census Service and confidentiality, 163
    data at Pittsburg, Kansas, center, 68
    questions, 141
    Services Department, 59
Personnel, Census, 70, 71. See also Census
    takers, Employees, Enumerators.
    adventures of, 160, 161
    selection of, 51

# Index

Petty, Sir William, and *The Anatomy of Ireland*, 25
Pittsburg, Kansas, personal data at, 68
Planning
  census use for, 226
  and DIDD, 227
*Political Arithmetick*, 25
Population
  center of, 99
  changes, factors affecting, 126, 127
  control, 133
  count, changes in types of, 73
  data, details on, 13, 63
  density, 98, 131
  difficulty in counting, 12
  effect on balance of power, 135
  ethnic groups in, 77
  explosion, future of, 131
  farm, changes in, 110
  growth, Civil War effect on, 43
  Growth Commission, 133
  immigration effects on, 131
  Indians in, 81
  moves, changes in, 89
  predicting, 43, 54, 128
  reflection, census as, 73
  religions of the, 83
  shifts, 75, 91
  Spanish-origin, 82
  theory and Thomas Malthus, 28
  underenumeration of, 12
  world, changes in, 132
  world, first estimate of, 26
*Portraits of France and Germany*, 24
Potter, Thomas, and English census, 76
Predictions, population, 128
*Present State of All Nations, The*, 24
Pretests for 1980 census, 203
Prices, data on, 118
Printed forms, first, 39
Printout of census tracts, 218
Privacy, 141
Processing
  the information, 215
  center in Jeffersonville, Indiana, 68
Program and Policy Development, 62
*Professional Careers in Census*, 71
Professional evaluation of census, 143
Protection of confidentiality, 144
Public
  Information Office, 62
  questions suggested by, 201
  use of records, 14
Publication
  programs of Bureau of Census, 66, 217
  of statistical tabulations, confidentiality protection in, 142

Publicity for census, 191, 204
Purchasing power, tracking, 119
Purpose of census, 11

Questionnaires, mailing, 57, 196, 214
Questions
  personal, 141
  selecting, 146
  suggested by the public, 201
  variety of, 146
Quinquennial census. *See* Five-year census.

Race categories in 1980 census, 204
Reasons
  for censuses, 16, 18, 20, 21, 22, 24, 26, 28, 30, 31
  for counting errors, 59
Records
  access to census, 14
  and Social Security numbers, 56
  storage in National Archives, 153
  stored, confidentiality of, 148, 153
Redistricting, state date for, 214
Refusal to answer penalty, removal of, 226
Regional offices, 68, 70
Registration, Survey of, 167
Rehearsal, dress, for 1980 census, 205
Religions and the census, 83, 226
Representation and census, 31
Research marketing, 191
Response
  burden in 1980 census, 210
  to census, 163
Responsibility, census, 144
Retail trade censuses, 67, 121
Revenue sharing, census data and, 198
Rickan, John, and reasons for census, 26
Roman census and Jesus, 20
Rome, ancient, census in, 19
Rules on confidentiality, 144
Russia, censuses in, 27, 57

Salmon, Thomas, and *The Present State of All Nations*, 24
Sampling, statistical, and Jacques Necker, 22
Sampling techniques, statistical, 10, 53
Second count, 217
Selected Service Industries, census of, 123
Shekel census, 17
*Six Books on the Commonwealth*, 24
Slaves in the census, 45
Social Security numbers and census records, 56
South America, census in, 30
Spain, first census in, 27

239